DESTINY STARTER™

HOW TO DISCOVER WHAT YOU ARE CALLED TO DO AND DO IT!

Anita "AC" Clinton

anita clinton

BE GREAT
Global

MY FREE GIFT TO YOU!

The ultimate goal for me is to see you fulfilling the *Call* on your life. Therefore, I've created the *Destiny Starter™* system to assist you along the way.

Be sure to download your FREE copy of the *Destiny Starter™ Workbook*. It will come in handy as you walk through the book.

In addition to the workbook, you get this FREE BONUS: **Destiny Stater™ Mini-Course**. It is the precursor to the full *Destiny Stater™ Digital Course* and *12-week Live Masterclass*. It includes 4 videos with worksheets that coincide with the first marker in the book and workbook.

<u>But wait there's more...</u>

There are a number of tools and resources that I've researched and recommend to further assist on your journey to fulfilling the *Call*.

<u>ACCESS THEM TODAY:</u>

www.destinystarterbook.com/extras

Anita Clinton Enterprises, LLC

Milwaukee, WI

ISBN 978-1-7350907-0-2: Hardcover
ISBN 978-1-7350907-2-6: Paperback
ISBN ISBN: 978-1-7350907-1-9: E-book
LCN 2020913891

First Edition: August 2020

Book designed by Anita "AC" Clinton
Book edited by Mich Nicolas

Published by Anita Clinton Enterprises, LLC
www.destinystarterbook.com
www.begreatglobal.com
www.anitaclinton.com

ACKNOWLEDGEMENTS

Special thanks to my mom Mary Clinton, brother Alex Clinton, late auntie Epper Miller, late uncle Joe Miller and aunt Annie Clinton for supporting and encouraging me in every dream, vision, and goal that I have had over the years. I also would like to thank Angel Johnson, Brandi Iberia Austin, Briana Melissa Myricks, Cecelia Marlow, Devona Wright Cottrell, Dorothy-Inez Del Tufo, Freddie & Krystal Taylor, Julissa Godinez, Kimberly R. Lock, La'Ketta Caldwell, Laneice McGee, Lashondra Scott, Liza Skinkis, Marki Lemons, Pat E. Perkins, Michael Thompson, Sydney Golliday, Tiffany Jordan, Torrence and Itaria Henry for all that you have poured into my life both personally and professionally.

I would also like to thank the ladies of SOAR for your support and encouragement.

Lastly, but definitely, not least, I would like to extend a special honorable mention to Peggy Flynn, Denisha Tate-McAlister, Dr. Michelle Majors, Chantell Sain, Adrienne J. Hunter, and Pastor Melva Henderson.

Peggy, thank you so much for coming into my life. You are one of the smartest and wisest people I know. I'm so grateful for you.

Denisha, thank you for being an amazing friend and the perfect example of a Virtuous Woman.

Michelle, I thank you for teaching me one of the most valuable lessons on acceptance and unconditional love.

Chantell Sain, thank you for being my friend and book club buddy. You are really unique, in that there aren't many people that I meet who truly get me, but you do on so many levels. And I am grateful for that and you.

Adrienne Hunter, girl, girl, girl...words cannot express how much you mean to me, my sister. I am profoundly grateful to have you in my life. Thank you for being my sounding board, my voice of reason, my sister girl. I have grown so much just by being around you. Thank you so much for all that you have brought to my life.

Pastor Melva Henderson, where do I start with you? First, you are an amazing woman. As I have shared with you several times, I'm in awe of your *Superpower*. Your commitment and determination to do what you were created to do are contagious...thank you for pouring into my life, for teaching me how to walk this journey the right way. Thank you for believing in and trusting me. Thank you for opening doors for me and giving me a chance. Thank you for impacting my life and the lives of thousands of other women and men. You represent God very well ma'am, very well indeed.

As I look back on all the people that have touched my life...I know for a fact that iron definitely sharpens iron, and I am so incredibly grateful for each you. There will always be a special place in my heart for you all and I sincerely pray many blessings upon you.

Yours Truly,

Anita "AC" Clinton

TABLE OF CONTENTS

MARKER THREE – EXECUTION: DO IT

MARKER FOUR – ACCOUNTABILITY: GROW IT

FOREWORD

I n a world where so many people are coming and going, it can be difficult to see who and what's authentic or fabricated. As an individual who's traveled the world meeting new people, I've learned not to pay much attention to movement, but rather, to impact. On rare occasions, someone comes in your midst and something within you takes note. The atmosphere changes and you realize *Greatness* walked into the room.

This was the case for me with Anita "AC" Clinton. Our initial meeting had me preoccupied with her physical stature; but with each encounter, my focus shifted because I recognized that her external would not compare to who she was internally. Anita is a leader. One who longs to see individuals moving toward their *Destiny*.

Many in the world talk about leadership, purpose, and empowerment, but few are willing to get their hands dirty helping someone else walk in it. I am honored to say Anita Clinton is one such individual. I have had the personal privilege of working one-on-one with her, and being a benefactor of her expertise and counsel. Somewhat clear in what I was *Called* to do, I had achieved a certain level of success and influence. I always understood that I was born to make a difference in the world. However, my first few meetings with Anita Clinton left me speechless. I knew meeting her would be a game changer for me as a leader. It quickly became obvious that I was working with someone who knew what she was doing and that her inner drive would push me to think deeper and reach further. Her valuable knowledge would help me take my leadership as well as my influence to the next level.

As she does in the book you are holding, Anita patiently walked with me. She simplified the *How*. *Destiny Starter*™ is a manual, a hands-on tool that can be read repeatedly, designed to take any determined person from where they currently are to where they long to be. *Destiny Starter*™ is packed with practical information and personal testimony that makes the book easily relatable. Anita candidly shares her personal journey of discovering her own *Purpose* amid a traumatic disappointment, which nearly ended her life.

At a time when many in the world are lost and struggling to find their place of significance, the timing of *Destiny Starter*™ is strategic. Everyone has been gifted and created in a unique way and through *Destiny Starter*™, Anita Clinton helps readers see that they were created to positively impact the world and that discovering their *Purpose* positions them for a lifetime of fulfillment.

Melva L. Henderson

Founding Co-Pastor of World Outreach Center (WOC)
Founder of World Bible Training Institute (WBTI)
Founder of World Ministerial Alumni Association (WMAA)
President/Director of Melva Henderson Ministries (MHM)
Author of The Practical Life Series, Faith Life Series,
and Fresh Baked Manna I and II

PREFACE

A life without Purpose leads to a life of unfulfillment, and in some instances, it can lead to destruction. – Anita "AC" Clinton

U nfortunately, you will never play again. Your career is over!" were the words on constant replay in her mind.

"*I can't believe this is happening to me! I have worked hard and poured everything into this sport. My entire life has been wrapped around basketball and without it, I am nothing. My life is ruined and no longer worth living!*" she said while lying incapacitated on her sofa.

In that moment, she had decided to end it all.

She had recently undergone reconstructive knee surgery and was given a strong medicine cocktail that she would use to execute her plan. While building up the courage, she began to eat the bunch of grapes stored in her refrigerator. When she had finished eating the grapes, she proceeded to say a small apologetic prayer and then take pill, after pill, after pill until most of them were gone. She laid down in tears and closed her eyes, with the intention of dying in her sleep.

She was a star athlete whose talent afforded her a full scholarship to a Big Ten University. Among various awards and accolades, she was privileged to win a bronze medal with the *William Jones Cup USA Basketball* team in Taipei, Taiwan.

However, her promising basketball career came to a halt when she experienced a traumatic knee injury. Up until this point, she believed that her persona and self-worth had been defined by her talent on the basketball court. And, after the injury crushed her dreams of becoming a professional athlete, she found herself lost and concluded her life was over and no longer worth living.

But there was a bigger *Purpose* for her life! Instead of going over to the other side, she woke up several hours later and her body began to regurgitate every pill she swallowed. It appeared the grapes she ate beforehand covered the lining and base of her stomach, providing a tightly sealed container that housed every single pill she swallowed. She arrived at the hospital several hours later where the doctors stated, based on the quantity and potency of the pills she took, it was truly a miracle that she was still alive.

⚙ ⚙ ⚙

So, you may be thinking, what does a suicide attempt story have to do with *Destiny* and fulfilling the *Call* on your life?

Excellent question! I'm a true believer that a life without *Purpose* leads to a life of unfulfillment, destruction and even death.

The particular scene above actually occurred in my life 20+ years ago. It was the catalyst that activated the personal search for my existence in this world. By all accounts I should be dead, but instead, my life was spared. In my determination to find out *Why*, my personal journey began.

What I found on my 20+-year journey is the essence of what I will share with those of you who are also searching for *Purpose*, fulfillment, and happiness in life. You may be close to or at the point I was during that pivotal moment in my life, or you may find yourself on the opposite end of the spectrum, diligently exploring, knowing that something's missing in your life but you are unable to pinpoint it. We all eventually find ourselves somewhere on that spectrum because we each inherently know that there should be more to our lives.

In fact, as we go through life, we are naturally drawn to our true *Calling*. It can be found in our dreams, goals, and desires. If it is true that only a small percentage of people transition into the realm they were created to operate in, then the majority of us never have the pleasure of even experiencing an iota of the *Greatness* that has been prepared for us. That is why it has been said that graveyards are full of unfulfilled dreams. This is an unfortunate reality that does not have to be.

It is possible to live an extraordinary life, filled with happiness and fulfillment – your dreams, your goals, your desires can be reality. Therefore, I want to challenge you to commit to pursuing them, and not to let them die with you when your time comes. If you would make this commitment today, this book promises to help you kickstart your *Destiny*.

BE GREAT GLOBAL (BGG)

1 BILLION DREAMERS WALKING BOLDLY IN THEIR GREATNESS AND TRANSFORMING THE FACE OF OUR WORLD

Throughout the book, you will read references to *Be Great Global* (BGG). BGG is an online training platform helping intrapreneurs and entrepreneurs answer the *Call* and love the work they do.

We envision a world where 1 billion morally conscious, ethical dreamers are walking boldly in their *Greatness* and transforming the face of our world. We believe that when you connect to the reason for your existence on earth, it not only changes your life, but it completely transforms what we all see and experience in the world. It's truly a game changer, and it matters – it really matters!

I can't stress it enough, the world (*we*) need what's inside of you!

Therefore, I want to personally invite you to come along on this journey of fulfilling the *Call* with me and other dreamers. You are already at the starting line because you are reading this book. I want to encourage you to not only start the journey but arrive at your destination. Don't stop, don't give up...you can do

BE GREAT GLOBAL (BGG)

this, and we are here to support you. So please take a moment and connect with us at www.begreatglobal.com.

On the website, you will find our podcast, online & offline training programs, and amazing resources needed to answer the *Call* on your life. To help you navigate through the site, be sure to visit our **Start Here** page.

For more information about BGG, visit www.begreatglobal.com.

From My Heart to Yours

LIVE EVERYDAY LIKE THERE'S NO TOMORROW

I woke up this morning with the mindset of living today like there's no tomorrow! At some point, we have all heard someone say, *"Tomorrow isn't promised to anyone."* So, I begin to think, when I die, on my tombstone, along with my name and some saying or Scripture, will be two dates separated by a dash.

The first date will be the year I was born, 1974, and the second date will be the year I died. But more important than any of that information is the little dash that separates those dates. You see, it is that dash that defines my life. It is not my name, the year I was born or the year I died, but that dash represents what I did during my time here on earth.

Now, it is crystal clear to anyone that knows me that I'm an adamant believer that everyone has a *Purpose*, a unique *Destiny*. We all were created to achieve *Greatness*, to have a dynamic impact on this world. And when it is all said and done – that dash between the dates on each of our tombstones should represent something special, something awesome, something greater than us. The world should be a better place simply because we were here.

So, if you are in alignment with me and believe that your dash should represent all that you were created to be – I challenge you to get serious about your *Purpose*, your unique *Calling* here on earth and join me by making a conscious decision to not only make your life count, but to live everyday like there's no tomorrow. Live everyday walking in your *Purpose*. Live every day, so that the little dash between the two dates on your tombstone exemplifies the impact that you had on this world, and the *Greatness* of our God who predetermined our destinies before we were born.

I will end with a quote by the legendary actor James Dean –

"Dream as if you will live forever, live as if you will die today!"[1]

– *Anita "AC" Clinton*

Introduction

INTRODUCTION

Our deepest fear is not that we are inadequate. Our deepest fear is that we are powerful beyond measure. We ask ourselves, who am I to be brilliant, gorgeous, talented and fabulous? Actually, who are you NOT to be?[2] – Marianne Williamson

I t has been said that there are four core things we all desire to know about ourselves:

1. Identity: Who Am I?
2. Lineage: Where Did I Come From?
3. Purpose: Why Am I Here?
4. Destiny: Where Am I Going?

This book is designed to help you answer the *Purpose* and *Destiny* questions. *(Note: I use the words Purpose and Call synonymously throughout the book.)* There's nothing like knowing why you exist and having a vision and plan for where you are going.

I believe that **now** is the time for us to experience life on the next level. You were created for *Greatness*. Your life should matter, your time on earth should be impactful. People should know you were here because of the impact your *Calling* had on making our world a better place.

THE CALL FOR GREATNESS

Several years ago, I co-hosted a youth empowerment seminar with approximately 50 high school students in attendance. As I started my presentation, I told them that they were created for *Greatness* – that they each possessed something inside of them that was designed to change the world. **I believe this statement to be true for everyone, including You!**

During my quest to determine the reason for my existence, I discovered that it was defined before I was born. The late internationally renowned best-selling author and speaker, Myles Munroe, expressed it like this: *"You came to this planet with an assignment to deliver to your generation. God looked into the future, foresaw a problem, and said 'I will create [add your name here] to solve this problem.'"*[3]

GREATNESS DEFINED

According to dictionary.com[4], *great(ness)* is defined as:
- a person who has achieved importance or distinction in a field
- of exceptional talents or achievements; remarkable
- doing or exemplifying (*a characteristic or pursuit*) on a larger scale

Napoleon Hill, author of *Think and Grow Rich*, defined *Greatness* as the ability to recognize the power of your own mind, embrace it, and use it.[5]

With a global population of over 7 billion, there are a plethora of challenges or problems impacting our world today. Let's take a moment and review the infographics on the next two pages...

The infographics portray a few of the larger challenges that we are facing as a society today.

Whether the challenge is large, medium, or small, guess what?

You, yes **you**, were created to solve at least one of today's challenges. You are a problem-solver. You were created for this moment in time, and the world is waiting on the manifestation of your *Greatness*.

And the best part of that is, not only are you well-equipped to solve the problem(s) – but your happiness and fulfillment in life are also found there. To put it clearly, you will **love** what you do!

How awesome is that? Now I can't speak for you, but that thought gives me goosebumps.

Global Challenges

1 OF 9 PEOPLE
In The World Suffer From
CHRONIC HUNGER

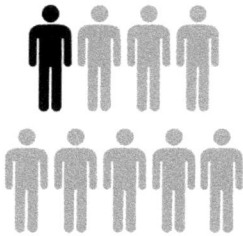

~38 MILLION
People Live With
HIV/AIDS

737 MILLION
People Live In
EXTREME Poverty

They Live On
$1.90/DAY

8 1 5 Million People

7.67 BILLION PEOPLE

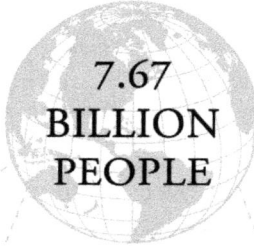

40 MILLION
Victims of Modern Slavery
GLOBALLY

750 MILLION
Adults Are Illiterate

464,000 HOMICIDES
Globally in 2017

$99 BILLION
Human Trafficking Industry

Sources:
Hunger Stats: Food and Agriculture Organization of the United Nations (FAO), www.fao.org, 2017.
HIV/AIDS Stats: www.hiv.gov, 2019. *Poverty Stats:* The World Bank, www.worldbank.org, 2015.
Homicide Stats: United Nations Office on Drugs and Crime. Global Study on Homicide, 2019. Austria:
United Nations Publication. Print. *Illiteracy Stats:* United Nations Educational, Scientific and Cultural
Organization. Literacy Rates Continue to Rise from One Generation to the Next. www.uis.unesco.org, Factsheet,
2017. Print. *Human Trafficking Stats:* International Labour Organization and Walk Free Foundation,
Global Estimates of Modern Slavery, 2014 & 2017. Print. *Population Stats:* United States Census Bureau,
www.census.gov/popclock, 2020.

American Challenges

1 OF 8
Americans Live In
POVERTY

40.6 MILLIONS
Americans

In 2018,
~1.7 MILLION
New Cases Of
CANCER
Diagnosed

1 OF 8
Americans Struggle
To Get Enough To
EAT

$41 MILLION
Americans

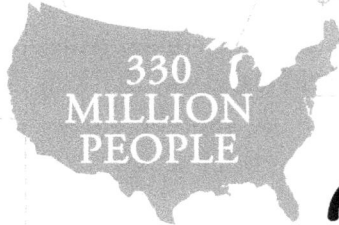

330 MILLION PEOPLE

US RANKS

Reading 24TH

Math 40TH

Science 24TH

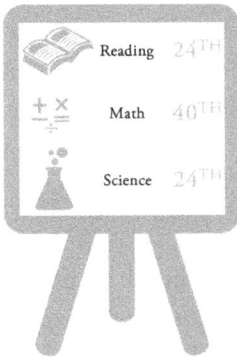

1.25 OF 3
US Adults Are Obese

~567,715
Americans Experience
Homelessness On A
Given Night

1 OF 5
Children 2-19
Are Obese

Sources:
Poverty Stats: Pew Research Center, www.pewresearch.org, FactTank, 2017. *Cancer Stats:* National Cancer Institute, www.cancer.gov, Statistics At A Glance, 2018. *Hunger Stats:* Feeding America, www.feedingamerica.org, Factsheet, 2017. *Obesity Stats:* CDC, 2019, www.cdc.gov/obesity/data. Homelessness Stats: Statista, *Estimated Number of Homeless People in the US, 2019, www.statista.com. Illiteracy Stats:* NCES, IES, U.S. Department of Education. *Performance of U.S. 15-Year-Old Students in Science, Reading, and Mathematics Literacy in an International Context,* 2016. Print. *Population Stats:* United States Census Bureau, www.census.gov/popclock, 2020.

But wait, you may be thinking – *how is that possible for someone like me?*

I recognize that we all come from different environments and have different external factors in our lives, but the fact of the matter is, it doesn't matter. Your ability to do something great has absolutely nothing to do with how much money you currently have, where you come from, your level or degree of education, whom you know or don't know, etc. Everything that you need to exercise *Greatness* in your life is already within you.

Additional training and development may be required to strengthen and enhance what you have, but the core of what you need is already there.

And, may I add, no one can do what you can do, like you can do it! There may be others doing similar things, but at the end of the day, they simply can't do it the way that you do it. There is no need to copy anyone else – just do **you**, the way you do **you**. The only thing that can stop or keep you from achieving *Greatness*, from impacting the world, is **you**.

Media mogul, Oprah Winfrey, simply stated it this way, "*You are responsible for your life. If you're sitting around waiting on somebody to save you, to fix you, to even help you, you are wasting your time. Only you have the power to move your life forward.*"[6]

LET THE JOURNEY BEGIN

This book is divided into four markers, each designed to take you step-by-step through the process of discovering, strategizing, and executing the *Call* on your life. It will provide the core tools and resources to help you walk boldly in your *Greatness* and fulfill your *Destiny*.

We will begin our journey with *Marker One–Discovery: Find It.* Here we will pinpoint that sweet spot where your Passion (*what you love doing)* meets your Genius *(talents, gifts, strengths)* meets Service *(to others)*. It is the thing(s) that puts you in your zone and sets the stage for **great** things to happen.

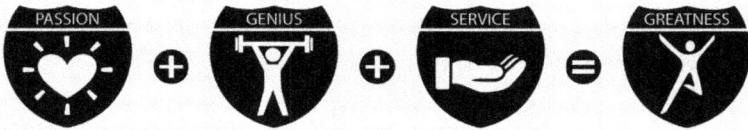

Passion + Genius + Service = Your Zone of Greatness (ZOG)

Once you have gained insight into your *Zone of Greatness (ZOG)*, we will transition to *Marker Two–Strategy: Plan It*. In this section, we will talk about *You*, and compose your *Who, Why, What, How, Where,* and *When*. Here you have an amazing opportunity to let your creative juices flow.

Then we will move into *Marker Three–Execution: Do It*. By the time we arrive here, you will have defined your ZOG, will clearly understand the vision, have a strategic action plan, and are ready to execute the plan.

And lastly, we wrap it all up with *Marker Four–Accountability: Grow It*. Here we will discuss viable options for accountability, support, and resources to help you along the way. The goal is to provide everything you need to kickstart your *Destiny*.

HOW TO READ THIS BOOK

As you read through the book, I recommend that you read each chapter in its entirety, and then do the activity for that chapter in the *Destiny Starter™ Workbook*. Once you have completed the activity, then continue to the next chapter and follow the same process.

For your convenience, there is a 45-day calendar or timeline in the *Destiny Starter™ Workbook*. It is designed to track your progress for 45 days, 2 hours a day. You determine how many days per week you can commit to working on your *Call*. For instance, if you can commit to 5 days a week, 2 hours a day, then you will be done in roughly 2.25 months. However, if you can only commit to 3 days a week, 2 hours a day, then it will take you roughly 3.75 months to complete. Whatever amount of days/hours per week you decide, I highly recommend that you stick to it until completion. You will notice that I have allocated time for *Review and Reflections* throughout the calendar. You can use those days to review, reflect and/or to catch up if you missed a day during the week.

Lastly, please know that this is a process requiring time and effort on your end. However, I promise that the benefits you obtain from this journey are absolutely invaluable.

THE DESTINY STARTER™ ROADMAP

To help paint a visual picture of the journey, I have created the *Destiny Starter™ RoadMap* that we will use throughout the book...

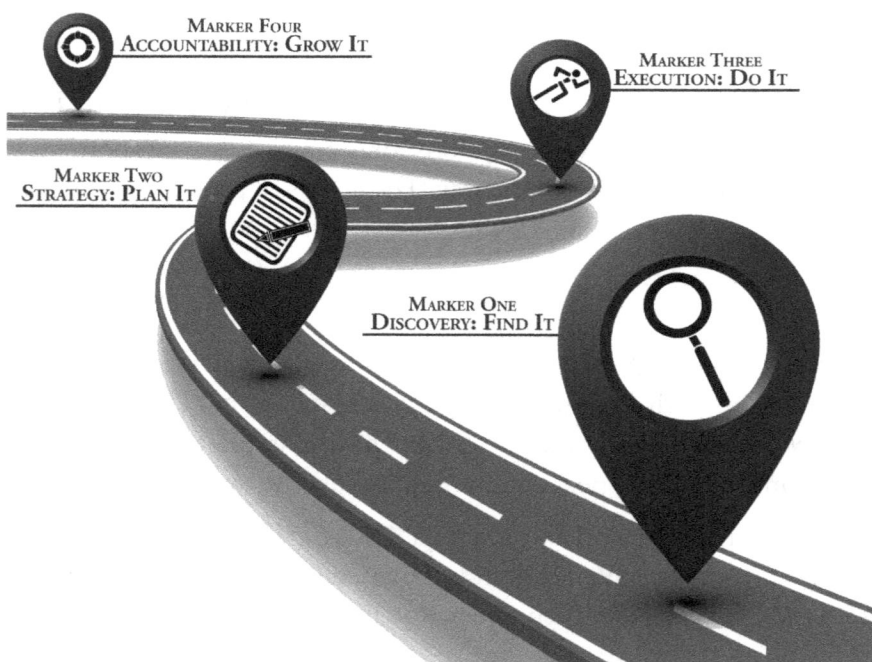

✎ BOOK COMPANION RESOURCES

In order to assist you along the way and to give you more direct guidance, I have created four companion resources:

1. **Destiny Starter™ Workbook.** The workbook is my **free** gift to you. It is designed to enhance your experience with this book. At the conclusion of most chapters, you will find an Activity reference for the workbook. These activities help you think through and record your thoughts and ideas. Also, the workbook provides additional tools and resources to guide you along the way.

2. **Destiny Starter™ Training Program.** The training program walks you through the 4 markers of the book, allowing you the opportunity to elevate your understanding and application of the book. The training program is offered in a DIY digital course, as well as a live virtual 12-week masterclass. You will receive 12 power-packed lessons, the course workbook and, depending on which level you choose, you will have access to our private group. It is an opportunity for you to meet and engage with other dreamers and game-changers. In addition, it is a place to ask questions, obtain feedback on thoughts and ideas, and be inspired and encouraged to get started or keep progressing forward.

3. **Be Great Global Podcast.** The podcast is designed to further motivate, inspire, and support you on your journey to fulfilling the *Call*. Every week we feature *how-to's*, relevant resources, case studies, and/or real-life interviews with *dreamers* who have transitioned to *game-changers*.

4. **BG Squad.** The *BG Squad* is our online community where you are among the first to receive our monthly resource giveaways and other goodies designed to help you fulfill the *Call*. I want to encourage you to get connected and sign up today for the *BG Squad*.

For more information and to download your FREE .pdf copy of the workbook, be sure to visit our website:

www.destinystarterbook.com/extras

SHARE YOUR SUCCESS

I would love to hear how this book and *Be Great Global* (BGG) are impacting your life. Not only am I interested in your story, but I'm sure that it will help

SHARE YOUR SUCCESS

many others get on track as well. Also, if you have questions, please don't hesitate to forward them to me and I will answer them on an upcoming podcast. I look forward to hearing from you.

www.destinystarterbook.com/share

From My Heart to Yours

JUST BE YOU!

Oftentimes, we consume ourselves with trying to please others – being the person that our parents want us to be, who our significant others or friends think we should be, who society tells us to be.

For the women, if we are aggressive and straightforward, we endure negative labels. For the men, if you express any emotion, God forbid you shed a tear, then you are considered weak, a punk.

In response, we find ourselves suppressing our true identity and/or sometimes we choose to live double lives. Either way, we rob ourselves of true happiness and live less than our best life.

So, in the words of Dr. Seuss – *"Be who you are and say what you feel, because those who mind really don't matter and those who matter really don't mind."*[7]

And I say, wake up and realize that you are fearfully and wonderfully made. Only you can be the best you. And check this out – when you accept who you truly are, miraculously so will others. At the end of the day, the world will see you exactly how you see you. With that, I want you to know, it's OK to just be you!

– Anita "AC" Clinton

Marker One

DISCOVERY: FIND IT

OVERVIEW:

FIND IT

If you really want to do something, you will find a way. If you don't, you'll find an excuse.[8]
– Jim Rohn

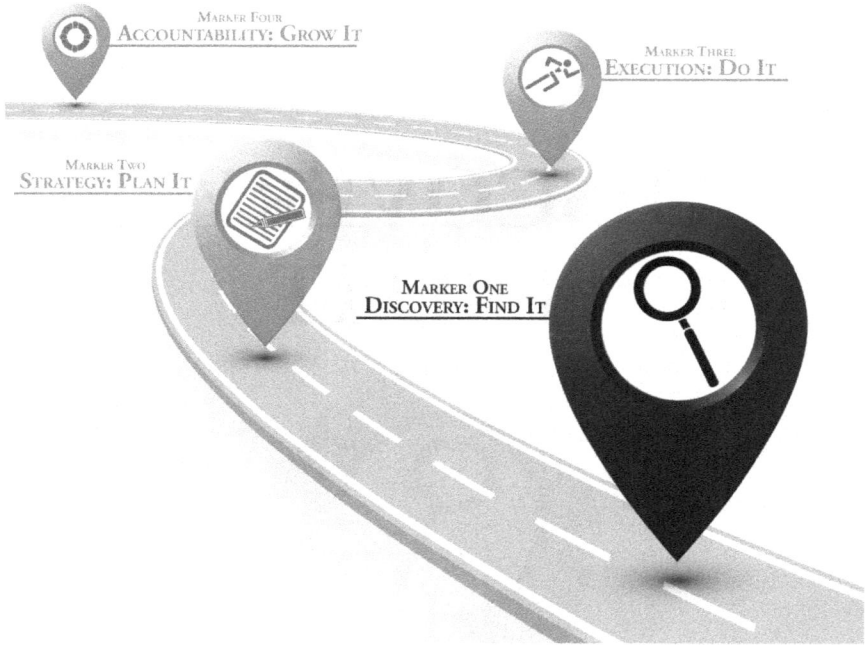

MARKER FOUR
ACCOUNTABILITY: GROW IT

MARKER THREE
EXECUTION: DO IT

MARKER TWO
STRATEGY: PLAN IT

MARKER ONE
DISCOVERY: FIND IT

Well alright, I hope you are as excited as I am about this amazing journey you are embarking on. I want you to know this is an initiative worthy of acknowledgement, and I take my hat off to you. Kudos!

Here we have arrived at the first marker on the *Destiny Starter™ RoadMap* called *Discovery: Find It*. It is the first step toward doing that which you were created to do.

Before we dive deeper into this, take a moment and think about the world's fascination with superhero, adventure, action-type movies. We love them!

In 2019, collectively they yielded over $1 trillion at the box office. *Avengers: Endgame* and *Avatar* are the highest grossing movies of all times, grossing over $2 billion each.

Why is that?

I believe it's game recognizing game. We love these types of movies because we see *Greatness* in them, and we instinctively know that *Greatness* is the realm we were created to operate in. Therefore, in those superheroes, we see ourselves or where we should be! We all have at least one *Superpower* or, as I call it, *Zone of Greatness* (ZOG) that is designed to positively impact the world.

Your ZOG resides in the sweet spot where your Passion (*what you love doing*), Genius (*talents, gifts, strengths*) and Service (*to others*) intersect. It is the thing(s) that puts you in your **zone** and sets the stage for **great** things to happen.

Passion + Genius + Service = Your Zone of Greatness (ZOG)

Once identified, your ZOG leads you to your *Calling*. Many people confuse assignments with *Calling*, and I think it is vital to draw a clear distinction between the two. Brad Lomenick explained this distinction the best in his book, *H3 Leadership: Be Humble. Stay Hungry. Always Hustle.*

"...while your Calling expresses how you were built and what you were designed to do best, an Assignment is the way you live that out. Calling is made up of seasonal-purpose assignments. Assignments give evidence of Calling and Purpose through different seasons."[9]

Therefore, your *Calling* or *Purpose* will remain fairly constant *(maybe changing a little here and there)* throughout the course of your life. It is the reason you exist. It is *Why* you do what you do. On the other hand, your assignment is *How* you do what you do, and it will most likely vary over time.

For example, my *Calling* is to help others connect to their *Purpose*. One of my assignments is *Be Great Global (BGG)*. It is one way I am fulfilling the *Call* on my life. Under *BGG*, I write books, create training programs, and share valuable resources to those in search of *Purpose*.

You, too, have a *Calling* that will consist of at least one assignment.

Are you ready to discover what that is? It all starts with your ZOG. In the next three chapters, we will assist you in discovering your ZOG:

Chapter 1: What's Your Passion?

Chapter 2: Pinpoint Your Genius

Chapter 3: The Gift of Service

Without further ado, *come on, let's do this!*

DESTINY STARTER™ – WHAT'S YOUR PASSION?

CHAPTER ONE:

WHAT'S YOUR PASSION?

If you can't figure out your purpose, figure out your passion. For your passion will lead you right into your purpose.[10] *– T.D. Jakes*

T he first component of the *Zone of Greatness (ZOG)* formula is **identify your passions.**

Oprah Winfrey said, *"Passion is energy. Feel the power that comes from focusing on what excites you."*[11]

So, my question would be: *what excites you?*

It gives you fulfillment every time you do it. In most instances, just the thought of it can bring a smile to your face. You are willing to invest your time and make sacrifices for it. So, let's unpack this some more.

BURNING DESIRE

One important variable to consider when defining your passion is **burning desire.** The profound thought leader, Napoleon Hill, stated, *"There is one quality which one must possess to win, and that is definiteness of purpose, the knowledge of what one wants, and the burning desire to possess it."*[12]

In February 2007, when Forest Whitaker accepted the *Oscar* for Best Actor for his role in *The Last King of Scotland*, he stated, *"When I was a kid, the only way that I saw movies was from the backseat of my family's car at the drive-in. And it wasn't my reality to think I would be acting in movies, so receiving this honor tonight tells me that it's possible. It is possible for a kid from east Texas, raised in South Central L.A. in Carson, who believes in his dreams, commits himself to them with his heart, to touch them, and to have them happen. Because when I first started acting, it was because of my desire to connect to everyone. To that thing inside each of us. That light that I believe exists in all of us. Because acting for me is about believing in that connection and it's a connection so strong, it's a connection so deep, that we feel it. And through our combined belief, we can create a new reality."*[13]

For Forest Whitaker, inside his *Purpose* is his burning desire to connect to people. Consider the characters he has played – a modern-day Samurai warrior-philosopher, a White House butler, a terrifying African dictator, a kidnapped British soldier, a troubled jazz saxophonist.[14] Now couple that with his acting style and ability to draw you into a character in a way that fuels sympathy and compassion for them. He brilliantly portrays each character in a way that leaves his audience intrigued and wanting more. Clearly, the desire he referenced is directly linked to his *Purpose*, manifested through acting, and has carried him to the top of his field.

When I think about my *Purpose*, I'm reminded of the fact that I've always wanted to help people overcome their challenges. If opportunities to help others were presented, I was always willing to be of service. I am naturally hardwired to fix it! Inside my desire to help others, I noticed that new talents were always unleashed.

I can remember when I was about seven or eight years old, my cousin needed help with his homework assignment. The assignment called for him to create an image of something that was important to him. Well my cousin loved cars, so he decided that he would draw one of his favorite *Matchbox Cars*. He went through several sheets of paper, trying to draw the car. Eventually, he gave up and started to cry. My heart went out to him and I felt compelled to help. When he had walked away, I picked up the paper and pencil, and begin to draw the car.

Now recognize that I had never really expressed much interest in drawing before this. However, approximately 30-minutes later, I had drawn the car on the paper. I called my cousin and he was so excited. He sat down, colored the car, added some wording, and his project was complete.

Everyone in my family was mesmerized at what I had accomplished with very little effort. It was through my burning desire to help my cousin that I was able to create for him the thing that he thought was impossible.

So, when we talk about burning desire, we all possess it. It is the thing that no matter what, we always gravitate to. Whether it is a desire to help and connect with others, build or create things, teach or sing, etc. – it is inside each of us. However, it takes individual action to get the ball rolling. There is a process, and stay tuned, we will dive deeper into it later in the book.

COMPENSATION'S OPTIONAL

Another important component to consider when defining your passion is **compensation's optional**. Dr. Martin Luther King, Jr. once said, "*We are prone to judge success by the index of our salaries or the size of our automobiles, rather than by the quality of our service relationship to humanity.*"[15]

So, what does compensation's optional mean?

It simply means that your passion involves that thing that you would do whether you were compensated or not. That's not to say that you aren't compensated for it, but that you don't necessarily attach a dollar amount to it simply because you enjoy doing it. Therefore, your passion involves that thing that you would do free of charge if necessary.

For example, I have a friend who once stated that her greatest pleasure and achievement in life was being a mommy. It is the thing that she enjoyed, excelled at, and didn't expect payment for. Now I know what you are thinking, *most mothers would say that.* But in all truth, she really is an excellent mom. Just watching her interact with her children, or anyone's child, is amazing.

At the time, she had three little ones around the same age and she never seemed to get tired of being with them. Not that they didn't push her buttons on occasion, but even in those moments, she still wanted to be around them. I know you've seen moms who are worn out and appearing in much need of a break. The fact of the matter is parenting, working with children is not an easy job and for her it was completely natural.

So, am I suggesting that her true *Calling* in life is being a mother?

Well, yes and no – I believe that many people are *Purposed* to be parents. However, I believe for many, knowing how to be a good parent is a skill that must be learned. Being a good parent doesn't come naturally to everyone – in my opinion, that is one of the reasons we have so many disturbed and lost children, teenagers, and even adults in this world today. So, in my friend's case, maybe her true *Calling* in life (*outside of being an exceptional mommy*) is to help or teach other women how to be exceptional mothers.

I think about all the babies having babies. If their parents aren't there to help out, who is teaching them how to raise their children?

What about those who had bad parenting, what positive influences do they have to help them be better parents?

What about mothers who have lost their children to child protective services and are seeking to get them back?

I could go on and on here, but the point is that this service is definitely needed in our society, and my friend has the experience, and most importantly, the skill set.

I have another friend who volunteers a lot of his time as a youth basketball coach. He spends multiple hours a week with youth athletes and compensation is not a factor. He does it because he is good at it and he enjoys it. His satisfaction comes in knowing that he was able to use his ZOG to help someone else.

We all know people who devote their time and life to youth sports' programs. In most cases, they are volunteering and spending their own money to make it happen. Their compensation is the fulfillment they get seeing the players excel and knowing that they were able to make a difference in the lives of our youth.

In fact, there are millions of people around the world who volunteer their time, using their gifts and talents to help and work with others. They understand the importance of giving back or sowing good seed into society. When we combine the willingness to sow or volunteer with our genius – our true *Calling* is in the midst.

With that, I want to reiterate that although you may be currently volunteering or willing to sow a seed to do the thing you are passionate about, it doesn't mean that you struggle doing it with no compensation or resources. That's absolutely not the case. As you operate in excellence inside your *Purpose*, financial increase and resources are the byproduct of the *Call*. And, anything that's done in excellence will automatically yield an increase – and that increase includes money.

Now does that mean, that getting money should be your top priority?

Absolutely not! Your top priority should be your assignment(s) inside the *Call*. Don't put seeking money or increase before the *Call*. It's about positively impacting people, and not fame, fortune, money or power. As you prepare to fulfill your *Destiny* please remember, increase follows the *Call*, and not the other way around.

EXAMPLES OF PASSION

Later in the book, we will discuss the *Who, What, When, Where, Why* and *How*. But for now, I want to introduce a part of that concept. The thing that you are passionate about is directly linked to *What* you are *Called* to do.

When it comes to me, my passions include: writing, speaking, teaching/training, researching, reading, and creative designing. So my question for you would be:

What are you passionate about?

To assist you with this process, here are some examples of passion:

Acting	Collecting Items	Cooking
Empowering Others	Exercising	Fishing
Investing	Knitting	Making Jewelry
Playing Instruments	Playing Sports	Photography
Reading	Scrapbooking	Sewing
Shopping	Singing	Teaching
Traveling	Vehicle Restoration	Writing

✍ DESTINY STARTER™ WORKBOOK

Need help defining your passion? See Activity One (1) in the *Destiny Starter™ Workbook* and complete the *Passion Test*. Don't overthink it. Pay close attention and record what immediately comes to mind.

CHAPTER TWO:

PINPOINT YOUR GENIUS

Genius is present in every age, but the men [or women] carrying it within them remain benumbed unless extraordinary events occur to heat up and melt the mass so that it flows forth.[16] *– Denis Diderot*

The second component inside helping you discover your *Zone of Greatness (ZOG)* is **pinpointing your genius.** Genius, as defined by *Oxford Dictionary*, is *"the exceptional intellectual or creative power or other natural ability."*[17] It is the natural talent or gift that you were equipped with from the very beginning of your existence, in addition to the core competencies, skills and knowledge that you have acquired over time. It is the ability to do something: sing, speak, write, teach, etc.

As Albert Einstein stated, *"Everybody is a genius. But if you judge a fish by its ability to climb a tree, it will live its whole life believing that it is stupid."*[18] Think about that for a moment: a fish is in its element when in water. There, it knows how to maneuver, it can do some amazing things. Take that same fish out of its environment and lean it against a tree, the talents and skills that it displayed while in the water are null and void. The fish is now useless.

The same is true for you and me. Outside of our environment, we are useless; but put us in our element and our genius is on full display. And when that genius is combined with passion and service, it is brilliantly designed for ease of use in fulfilling our Destiny and walking boldly in our *Greatness*. So, let's dive a bit deeper into this concept.

EFFORTLESS

The most important variable in pinpointing your genius is that it is **effortless**, or it comes easy to you. Now understand that effortless does not mean you don't work. I know you've heard the saying *anything worth having, you must work for it.* The task at hand may require your time, but it will be as natural as the unconscious blinking of your eyes. And you will achieve results.

Let me give you an example – most of us are familiar with the story of David and Goliath. According to man's standards, of all Jesse's sons, David was the least likely to be considered **the one** to be the King of Israel. However, not only was he the chosen one, but he had also been equipped to handle the task at hand. This is clearly evident in his defeat of the giant, Goliath. By all accounts, Goliath should've crushed little David. However, through his courage, determination, preparation, and faith, not only was the giant defeated, but it was destroyed with very little effort on David's part. Before Goliath realized what had happened, his face was hitting the ground.

OK, let's bring it a little closer to home with basketball greats: Larry Bird, Magic Johnson, Michael Jordan, Kobe Bryant, and Lebron James. If you were to really zoom in and watch their movement and actions on the court, you will clearly see how they operate with sheer ease. There is no struggle, it is a natural occurrence for each of them. Watching them play is like viewing the natural flow of water moving downstream. In comparison to that flow, your genius on full display is just as smooth.

When you are truly walking in your *Calling*, you will notice that everything you need is already inside you or within arm's reach. As you move forward, you will recognize that you can do things that you may not have thought possible. You may find new talents that you didn't even know existed and if additional things are needed, the right people will cross your path to assist you.

EXAMPLES OF GENIUS

Everybody is a genius, and like passion, it too is linked to your *What*. My genius entails my abilities to write, teach/train, speak, think strategically, research, and create graphics/websites. So here, my question for you would be:

What is your genius?

As we did before, I would also like to share some examples of genius *(the ability to...)*:

Create Graphics	Create Music	Draw
Evangelize	Exhort	Farm
Fish	Heal	Lead
Make People Laugh	Manage Finances	Motivate
Negotiate	Network	Organize
Produce Videos	Recruit	Research
Sew	Sing	Speak
Teach	Think Strategically	Write

❋　❋　❋

Once you've pinpointed your genius, take a moment and answer this question: *How does your genius align with the things you are passionate about?*

For instance, if singing is your passion – can you sing acapella? How is the pitch and tone of your voice? Are you asked to lead songs or sing solo at gatherings and events? If we posted a video of you singing on social media, would the popular view and opinion be favorable? If the answers to these questions are yes, then you may be on the right path. However, if the answer is no, what talents, skills, and knowledge do you have that will be impactful in the singing/entertainment industry or field? (i.e., *Can you write songs, create music or beats, produce and master tracks, etc.?*) The point here is, although singing may not be your genius, it doesn't mean that your *Calling* isn't in the entertainment industry, if that's what you are passionate about. You just need to figure out what genius you possess to operate in that field.

The objective here is to link your passions with your genius.

SHARPEN YOUR GENIUS

As I stated previously, you have been equipped with what's needed to fulfill the *Call*. However, it is important to recognize that your genius may need to be fine-tuned and perfected.

Remember the story with my cousin and his homework assignment that I shared in the previous chapter. Before that period, I had never expressed much interest in drawing. However, when the talent was needed, it manifested and yielded results. My aunt took notice and began to encourage me to draw more. As I got older, she enrolled me in art school, which helped me to sharpen that talent.

Fast forward to today, creative design is a huge part of what I do to help others develop the brand identity for their vision. It is the exact talent that sprouted years ago with my urge to help my cousin with his project, and today, I'm using that honed talent to assist people in fulfilling the *Call* on their lives.

Let's explore another example. In my basketball days, playing the sport came natural to me. However, I still had to practice enhancing my skill level – the more I practiced, the better I became. The natural talent that I possessed, coupled with intentional practice, is the reason I had the opportunities to travel across the *United States* playing basketball. It is the reason I was privileged to play with *USA Basketball* and win a bronze medal in *Taipei, Taiwan.*

If your genius needs to be fine-tuned and perfected, there are a number of options to consider like going back to school with an emphasis on where you want to go. For instance, if one of your goals includes advancing to upper management or the C-suite (*CEO, CFO, CIO, CMO, etc.*), maybe getting a MBA is the target.

If you are looking to become a project manager, maybe a project management certification program would be beneficial.

I personally completed an *Entrepreneurship Certification* from *Cornell University's* online education department, and I'm interested in getting my *Six Sigma Certification.* Both of these are beneficial for what I do.

Reading or listening to books and attending conferences are other great sources for growth and development. The ultimate goal should be reading books or attending events with the intent to apply what you've learned.

All the above typically require a financial investment, but if you are looking for free options, you can start with tutorials on *Google* and *YouTube* university. There are tutorials and videos that cover just about every topic imaginable.

In addition, there are internships or volunteer opportunities where you can learn or practice your craft.

Let me give you another example. I grew up in church, and when I first started speaking, I went to the arena and environment that I knew, and made it known that I was interested in speaking. I took any and every opportunity to speak that was available to me, no matter how small or big.

And guess what, the better I got, the more opportunities I received, and that led to other opportunities like doing workshops, conferences, and other events outside my church. I also started a podcast, which helped me get comfortable communicating on a consistent basis. I used what was in my reach to hone my skills, and then from there launch my speaking career.

Today, I'm always open to opportunities that will enhance the skill sets needed for me to walk in my *Purpose*. No matter how small the opportunity, if I can see the potential for growth, I take it on. *(See the Destiny Starter™ Workbook for additional resources.)*

DO IT IN EXCELLENCE

Based on the genius you pinpointed, position yourself to do it in excellence! And by excellence, I mean, extremely good, great, outstanding. When you begin to walk in your *Calling*, excellence should be the standard. And anything done in excellence, people are willing to pay a premium price for it.

Look at *Apple* products...it is estimated that there are over 700 million *iPhone* users in the world.[19] *Apple* customers stand in line for days to be among the first to get the latest *iPhone*. That's just one product; we won't even speak about the numbers for their other products.

Why? *Apple* products are done in excellence, all the way down to the packaging. Upon purchase of an *Apple* product, it comes in a simple, yet elegant box with clean graphics and font. You open the box and each component is perfectly wrapped and positioned in its own compartment. The product design is slick and unique. You power on the product and there's even more magic. The developers have taken the time to work through the entire user experience from start to finish. *Apple* does what they do in excellence, and 700+

million *iPhone* users are willing to pay the premium price tag to own the product.

I repeat, anything done in excellence, people are willing to pay a premium price. Don't settle for mediocrity; be the best at what you do.

Therefore, if training and development are needed, I encourage you to be open to the opportunities that are all around you to sharpen your skill sets. These opportunities may be on your job, at your church or local community organizations. They may even be found amongst your family and friends. Get creative, open your eyes and you will see them. Trust me, they are already there!

With that in mind, take some time to pinpoint possible opportunities that can help you develop the natural skill sets that you already possess.

✎ DESTINY STARTER™ WORKBOOK

See Activity Two (2) in the *Destiny Starter™ Workbook* to narrow down your genius, as well as think through and record potential opportunities to help you sharpen that genius.

CHAPTER THREE:

THE GIFT OF SERVICE

I don't know what your destiny will be, but one thing I do know: the only ones among you who will be really happy are those who have sought and found how to serve.[20] – Dr. Albert Schweitzer

I will start this chapter proposing a question: *Where do we learn selfishness – is it something we are taught or are we born with it?*

Think about asking a toddler for something he or she has. The majority of them will say *"no, it's mine"* and even if they can't talk, they understand how to communicate *"no."* Usually, the ones who will share are those whose parents have taught them to share.

Let's keep it real: selfishness is running rapid in our world today.

If we look at social media, it is projected that millions of selfies *(self-portraits)* are taken and posted on the internet every day.[21] As a society, we are consumed with self – oh wait – look at me!!! We tend to be so concerned about self that we neglect to consider how what we do or say impacts others. I have definitely been guilty of this!

It is my belief that selfishness can detour us from reaching our *Destiny!* We were created to help each other, and this is the basis of the third component inside discovering your *Zone of Greatness* (ZOG): **service to others.**

Service is all about impact. Whatever it is that you are on this earth to do, it's about making life better for other living beings (*i.e, humans, animals, birds, insects, plants, trees, etc).*

REAL-LIFE EXAMPLES OF GREATNESS

So, let's look at some of the world's most influential people who have discovered their ZOG and took action. And as a result, their presence on earth has made a difference, and their impact on our world is undeniable:

Bill Gates[22]

As we look ahead into the next century, leaders will be those who empower others. – Bill Gates

Bill Gates, founder of *Microsoft*, is one of the most influential and richest people in the world today. Millions of people across the world use *Microsoft's* computer operating software daily. A thought, a passion, a *Purpose* that started in a garage has spread and impacted society as a whole.

In addition, his success with Microsoft opened the door for *"The Bill and Melinda Gates Foundation."* The foundation has sought to focus on global issues ignored by the government and improving the standards of public school education in the United States.

In addition, the foundation provides a trustworthy platform for over 150 billionaires to invest a sizable percentage of their earnings. This effort has been spearheaded by billionaire Warren Buffett, who has committed to sowing a significant percentage of his earnings to the foundation.

George Washington Carver[23]

No individual has any right to come into the world and go out of it without leaving behind him distinct and legitimate reasons for having passed through it. – George Washington Carver

It has been said that George Washington Carver was a dynamic man, who communicated one-on-one with God inside his laboratory to create over 300 products from peanuts, and over 100 products from sweet potatoes. Carver's life spanned 1864-1943 *(from the Civil War to World War II)*. He suffered through an extremely difficult period for African Americans, 1864-1896, reconstruction and Jim Crow.

He was born into slavery, denied entry into several schools, and had to push and persevere through many obstacles, hardships, and challenges to leave his mark on the world. He was eventually able to attend school, earn his master's degree, and become a [professor] at the Tuskegee Institute – a trade school for blacks in Alabama.

As stated on cbn.com by Tyrone Brandyburg of the *Carver Museum*, *"Carver believed that the Great Creator gave him – or at least allowed him – to do these things or have these skills."* Carver himself stated, *"When I was young, I said to God, 'God, tell me the mystery of the universe.' But God answered, 'that knowledge is for me alone.' So, I said, 'God, tell me the mystery of the peanut.' Then God said, 'Well, George, that's more nearly your size.'"* As a result, Carver was able to co-create hundreds of products with God.

Through it all, his faith in God and his willingness to humble himself opened unimaginable doors of opportunity for him independent of the barriers. Below are a select few of the products that he created:

• Peanut Butter	• Dyes for Leather/Clothes	• Diesel Fuel
• Peanut Haymeal	• Wood Stains/Paints	• Marble
• Laundry Soap	• Glue	• Plywood
• Rubbing Oil	• Plastics	• Linoleum
• Hand/Face Lotion	• Ink	• Charcoal
• Shampoo		• Pancake Flour

Henry Ford[24]

A business absolutely devoted to service will have only one worry about profits. They will be embarrassingly large. – Henry Ford

Henry Ford was an industrialist who changed the face of automobile manufacturing in America. Despite being labeled ignorant and uneducated, through his *Purpose*, his inventions and concepts of efficient mass production revolutionized transportation and changed the automobile industry. The outcome of his dreams, passion, determination, and *Purpose* made him one of the wealthiest men of his time and continues to impact the entire world to this day.

Dr. Martin Luther King Jr[25]

I have a dream that one day this nation will rise up and live out the true meaning of its creed: We hold these truths to be self-evident: that all men are created equal. I have a dream that one day on the red hills of Georgia the sons of former slaves and the sons of former slaveowners will be able to sit down together at a table of brotherhood. – Dr. Martin Luther King Jr.

Dr. Martin Luther King Jr. was one of America's most influential civil rights' activists. His passionate but nonviolent protests helped to raise awareness of racial inequalities in America. His mission led to significant political changes for African Americans in the U.S. Dr. King was also an eloquent orator who captured the imagination and hearts of people of all races. His *Purpose* essentially impacted the lives of millions of people and drastically changed the world.

Mother Teresa[26]

I have found the paradox that if I love until it hurts, then there is no hurt, but only more love. – Mother Teresa

Mother Teresa was an internationally recognized humanitarian whose life changed the way we thought about the world around us. Through her unselfish acts of love, she became an agent of change. She taught us that everyone, regardless of wealth, health, social standing, religion, sex, or creed, has value in the eyes of God. And the greatest way to show His love is through meeting the needs of others.

Oprah Winfrey[27]

I don't think you ever stop giving. I really don't. I think it's an ongoing process. And it's not just about being able to write a check. It's being able to touch somebody's life. –
Oprah Winfrey

As stated in Oprah Winfrey's biography, through the power of media, she has created an unparalleled connection with people around the world. As the former supervising producer and host of the top-rated, award-winning *The Oprah Winfrey Show*, she entertained, enlightened, and uplifted millions of viewers for two decades. Her accomplishments as a global media leader and philanthropist have established her as one of the most respected, influential, and admired public figures today.

In 1997, Oprah created *Oprah's Angel Network* that sponsors charitable initiatives worldwide. The network is dedicated to inspiring people to make a difference in the lives of others.

In 2007, she opened the *Oprah Winfrey Leadership Academy for Girls*, a $40-million school that provides educational and leadership opportunities for academically gifted girls from impoverished backgrounds in South Africa who exhibit leadership qualities for making a difference in the world.

Today, Oprah's *OWN* television network creates original TV programming, including the *Emmy Award* winning *Oprah's Lifeclass, Iyanla: Fix My Life*, and *Super Soul Sunday*.

* * *

I could highlight hundreds and thousands of other people to support the argument that our *Destiny* is not for our individual benefit, but for positively impacting others. Just as with the people highlighted above, when you are truly walking in your *Purpose* – the impact can be felt around the world, touching the lives of many.

However, here's the beauty of it: If reaching the world doesn't appeal to you, then that's OK, too. You can choose to go as far out there as you want to go, keep it local, or do nothing at all. There are no limitations or boundaries; however, if you choose to accept the mission, the impact will be felt and life-changing – it will be great!!!

For now, let's reflect on the passions and genius you identified in the previous chapters. I ask the question, *how does your passion and genius benefit or serve others?*

◉ ◉ ◉

When you get to this point, you should have at least one (1) concept that aligns with passion, genius, and service to others. If you have more than one concept that aligns, consider the overall connector among them that positively impacts others.

For instance, your passion and genius could entail cooking, exercising, and teaching, and when combined, the end result, is *helping people live healthy lifestyles.*

Essentially, you want to determine what's the end result of you doing things you love in excellence, are skilled at, and that positively impact others. This is your *Zone of Greatness (ZOG)* or *Superpower.*

◉ ◉ ◉

As we stated previously, the sweet spot where your passions, genius and service to others meet is your ZOG.

Whatever that thing is for you, the next step is to create what I call your ZOG *Statement.* This statement summarizes your passion, genius and service to others in one sentence. It can be used anytime someone inquires about what you do, you can use it on your social media profiles, in your email signature, on your resume, etc...as you will see later in the book, it has many uses. In addition, it becomes the confirmation that you have officially claimed the *Call* on your life.

For example, writing, speaking, teaching/training, researching, reading, and creative designing are my passions, I'm very skilled at doing them in excellence, and when I do them there is definitely a positive impact to others. Therefore, when I look at all of them collectively, the end result of using them *(my ZOG)*, is *helping others connect to their Purpose in life*. When I'm doing that, I'm in my **zone**, and **great** things always happen.

I've taken all of that in consideration to create my official ZOG *Statement* and it reads as follows: *I help intrapreneurs and entrepreneurs find happiness, fulfillment, and money doing work they actually love.*

I have created a template in the *Destiny Starter™ Workbook* to help you create your ZOG *Statement*. You will tweak and tweak, and tweak some more over time until you get to the perfect statement for you.

We will circle back to this in Part 2 of the next section.

At this point, you may not understand exactly what to do with this information. Don't worry, we will further unpack it as we walk through the upcoming chapters.

✎ DESTINY STARTER™ WORKBOOK

See Activity Three (3) in the *Destiny Starter™ Workbook* to finalize your *Zone of Greatness*. If you are unable to carry at least one (1) concept throughout – I highly recommend that you walk through Activities 1–3 again. In addition, you will find the template and keywords to help you create your ZOG *Statement*.

BRINGING IT ALL TOGETHER

A s we conclude *Marker One – Discovery: Find It* of the *Destiny Starter™ RoadMap*, let's review the three (3) key areas:

1. WHAT'S YOUR PASSION

The first component to identifying your *Zone of Greatness* is passion. It is directly linked to the thing that is burning in your heart. You are extremely passionate about it – doing it brings you peace and fulfillment. You are willing to invest your time and even make sacrifices for it. You are willing to do it whether you receive compensation or not. Even though that doesn't mean that you won't get compensated for it, because there is absolutely a value associated with doing it.

2. PINPOINT YOUR GENIUS

The second component to identifying your *Zone of Greatness* is genius. You have been equipped with natural talents or gifts, coupled with the core competencies, skills and knowledge that you have obtained over time - they all are to be used in service to the plan for your life. We all have at least one genius.

3. THE GIFT OF SERVICE

The final component to identifying your *Zone of Greatness* is service. We are all here to be of service to one another. Our *Purpose*, our *Destiny*, our *Calling* have very little to do with us, but everything to do with serving and benefiting others. The world desperately needs what's inside of you.

Once you are clear about those three (3) components, you have your *Zone of Greatness* (ZOG). In a nutshell, it is your ability to do something that you are passionate about and that positively impacts others.

For now, I ask you to take a couple of seconds and acknowledge the completion of *Marker One – Discovery*.

Congratulations!

This is an amazing milestone and I don't want to just breeze over it. So please do me a favor, smile, and pat yourself on the back. **WooHoo!!!**

NOW WHAT?

With your ZOG identified, next we dive into the *how-to*.

But before we go there, I challenge you to be intentional about taking on the opportunities you identified to sharpen your skills. The only way to perfect and/or strengthen them is through using them.

And remember this, **no one can do what you can do, like you can do it, so just do you!**

From My Heart to Yours

REASON, SEASON, LIFETIME

It has been said that people enter our lives for a reason, season, or lifetime. And I've found, we often cause ourselves unnecessary heartache and pain simply because we fail to distinguish between the three. So, let me help you out – I once heard Bishop T.D. Jakes[28] define these three (3) types of people the best.

He labeled the first type **The Confidant**. A confidant is that person or group of people who are for you and are for what you are for. They love you unconditionally, they laugh when you laugh, they cry when you cry. Essentially, they only want the best for you! They will be there for a lifetime.

He labeled the next type **The Constituent**. A constituent is the person or group of people who are for what you are for but not necessarily for you. They will connect with you because they are headed in the same or similar direction as you. They will work well with you, and together, you may even accomplish great things. But don't get it twisted, because they are not for you. If someone else or another opportunity comes along, they will drop you off to explore the other option. And they will take your secrets, your strategy, your plans with them when they leave. You see, they are just there for a season.

And finally, the last type he labeled **The Comrade**. A comrade is not for you, neither is that person or group of people for what you are for. Basically, they will connect with you because you each have a common enemy or barrier to overcome. They will strategize with you to defeat the enemy or tear down the barrier. However, once the reason they were there has been realized, their time with you is over.

Now understand, none of them necessarily represents a negative, because all three are needed for you to fulfill your *Destiny*. Yet it is vital that you recognize the character of each and that you interact with them accordingly.

So I leave you with this, treasure those who are there for a lifetime and rejoice in the time spent with those who are there for a season or reason, and when the time comes, you must be willing to let them go...

– Anita "AC" Clinton

Marker Two

Strategy: Plan It

OVERVIEW

PLAN IT

A goal without a plan is just a dream.[29] *– Dave Ramsey*

I am so jumping up and down, cheering profusely for you right now. We've made it through the first marker on the *Destiny Starter™ RoadMap*, and now the creativity begins...so let's do this!

This next marker, *Strategy: Plan It*, will be divided into two parts: *Part One: Let's Talk About You*, and *Part Two: Now, Let's Talk About Your Vision*.

There are a couple of personal areas that I highly recommend you reconcile before we can venture into your vision. I encourage you not to bypass this portion of marker two, because it is a crucial component.

We all have baggage, experiences from our past that impact our present, and oftentimes, halt our future. And when we talk about fulfilling the *Call*, if you fail to deal with the baggage up front, it will stifle your progress.

Once we have unpacked some key areas with you personally, we then direct our attention to your vision. In its simplest form, vision answers the question – *What's the future you aspire to create?*

I am a huge advocate of creating mission and vision statements for anything worth pursuing in life. I believe if you can mentally see where you are going and take the fear of failure off the table, you can actualize whatever it is you envisioned. And, when we talk about vision statements, it is your *Why* that answers the question: *Why does what you do matter?*

In this section, we will also unpack your:

- Who: *Who is your target audience?*

- What: *What can your target audience expect to receive from you?*

- How: *How will you share or deliver your message, product, service, or program?*

- Where: *Where will you be located – online, offline or both?*

- When: *When will you officially get started?*

As I mentioned previously, the *Call* on your life is not about you, but about positively impacting other living beings. We are called to be the salt of the earth and the light of the world. Among many uses, salt is widely known for its flavoring and preservative qualities. In addition, wherever there is light, darkness cannot exist. So, when we add it all up, our existence on earth should bring the flavor or essence and illumination of God, while preserving or maintaining its original state.

If you think about it, that's really **powerful!**

With that thought lingering, let's go ahead and jump into *Part One* of this section: *Let's Talk About You.*

From My Heart to Yours

THE POWER OF POSSIBILITY

Possibility is defined by *Webster* as *"the condition or fact of being possible."* The archaic definition is of *"one's utmost power, capacity, or ability."*[30] I must say that I love that definition – think about it, one's utmost power, capacity, or ability.

So, I ask, what is really possible in life?

According to the archaic definition, what's possible in each of our lives is based on our individual power, capacity, ability, and I will add belief. The Chinese thinker and philosopher Confucius said, *"The man who thinks he can and the man who thinks he can't are both right."*[31]

Now since I believe that everyone, including you, has a *Purpose* and that everything we need is already inside of us to fulfill that *Purpose* and achieve *Greatness* in life – my answer to the question, *"What is really possible in life?"* is anything within your utmost power, capacity, ability, and belief is possible for you. It may not be possible for anyone else, but it can be possible for you.

So, let's explore an example: Political activist, Nelson Mandela, was imprisoned for 26 years for opposing governmental apartheid, a system of legal segregation. After he was released in 1990, he made the decision to continue his life's work. In 1991, he was elected the first black President of South Africa, the home of apartheid. In 1993, he was awarded the *Nobel Peace Prize* for *"the peaceful termination of the Apartheid regime, and for laying the foundations for a new democratic South Africa."*[32]

Now despite the circumstances, Mandela believed in the possibility of an anti-apartheid governmental system. He was relentless in using his utmost power, capacity, ability, and belief to make that a reality.

There are many more examples that both you and I could pull. At the end of the day, you determine the possibilities for your life and at the same time, you determine the limitations in your life. You can go as far as you choose or not, based on your utmost power, capacity, ability, and belief.

So, I ask you again, what is really possible in your life?

– *Anita "AC" Clinton*

Part One:

Let's Talk About You

CHAPTER FOUR:

LIFE'S TRAINING OBSTACLES

What if everything you are going through right now is preparing you for a dream bigger than you can imagine? – Author Unknown

D r. Maya Angelou[33] became the first African American woman with a non-fiction book, *I Know Why the Caged Bird Sings*, on the best-sellers list in 1970. As a child, she lived partially with her mother in St. Louis and partially with her grandmother in Stamps, AK. At the age of eight she was raped by her mother's boyfriend while on a visit to St. Louis. After she testified against the rapist, several of her uncles beat him to death. Believing that she had caused the man's death by speaking his name, Dr. Angelou refused to speak for approximately five years. As she stated, *"I thought if I spoke, my mouth would just issue out something that would kill people, randomly, so it was better not to talk."*

Imagine that – Dr. Maya Angelou thought her words would randomly kill people when in actuality, it is her words that have blessed and positively impacted millions, if not billions, of people. As stated in her biography, *"Dr. Angelou's words and actions continue to stir our souls, energize our bodies, liberate our minds, and heal our hearts."*[34]

As we go through life, many of us face challenges, obstacles, and occurrences that have the potential to thwart our *Purpose*. But I'm here to say that everything you've gone through has prepared you for the *Call* on your life. Now let's be clear here, I am in no way saying that you **had** to go through what you've been through, but that it has prepared you.

Angelou wrote in one of her poems, *Still I Rise*: "*You may write me down in history with your bitter, twisted lies. You may trod me in the very dirt but still, like dust, I'll rise. Does my sassiness upset you? Why are you beset with gloom? 'Cause I walk like I've got oil wells pumping in my living room.*"[35]

When I look back over my life, I can remember growing up and it seemed that every time I would set out to help someone, I would get hurt. As stated previously, I have always had a heart to help others and as I purposed to be of assistance, it seemed my kindness would be taken advantage of. This resulted in me becoming a cold, mean, and selfish individual who built a huge wall to guard my heart. It took a lot to penetrate that wall, and those who got in and violated the privilege, would not be forgiven. In the end, I grew distant and very reluctant about helping others. In fact, I became emotionless toward most people.

Those experiences crushed my spirits, turned my open and caring heart cold, and then I could be of no effect to others. In that state, I could not and would not fulfill my *Purpose*.

FINDING PEACE WITH YOUR PAST

Whether you are aware of it or not, your way of *being*, how you show up in the world today, how you respond to situations or circumstances, the thought processes used to manage your life, are largely impacted by your past experiences. Oftentimes, we carry what happened to us at the ages of 5-10 around with us throughout our existence. Some of us wrap and package it in beautiful boxes and bags, while others leave it hanging out of worn and beat-up bags, and yet some wear them fully exposed on their sleeves. Either way, when the pressure arrives, it is guaranteed to burst out uncontrollably. And even though it could look different for each of us, the impact is still felt and is oftentimes destructive.

Let me give you an example of what I mean...

Growing up, I can pinpoint several key experiences that conformed my way of being in the world. I will share one of them with you here.

When I was a child, I was daddy's little girl. My father was kind, sweet, and attentive to me. I loved my dad, and in my eyes, he could do no wrong. However, at the time, I didn't know my dad had a serious drug addiction. When I was around the age of 5, my mother was fed up and asked him to leave our home. When he left and never came back, I was distraught. I was too young to really comprehend what was happening, but on some level, I knew I had been abandoned, and hatred toward my dad began to build.

When I got a little older, one day my mom explained that she asked my dad to leave because he refused to stop using drugs. Therefore, she decided that she didn't want me and my brother in that environment. Yet, what I heard was, *I wasn't good enough and my dad chose drugs over me.* That was the narrative that I used to construct my identity moving forward.

From that moment on, I set out to prove to everyone that I was **good enough**. I worked overtime to be an exceptionally great kid, teenager, and young adult. I rarely got into trouble because I was determined to make my family proud of me...and I did.

As I became an adult, that same narrative continued to play out in my life. I was always looking to prove my worth *(that I really was good enough)* to others. In fact, I was meticulous in all my personal and professional dealings. I always operated on a higher level, and I expected reciprocity from others.

Now because the expectations were set so high, very few people were able to meet them, and when they couldn't or I felt I wasn't being appreciated, I would immediately find the closest exit. As you can probably imagine, I ruined many friendships, relationships, and business partnerships along the way.

My love life was a disaster. Although I couldn't see it at the time, remnants of the hatred that had grown over the years toward my dad showed up in every romantic relationship I had. Those guys never had a chance because of my preconceived notions of who I thought they were. From my perspective, they each represented my dad who I could never satisfy and who would always leave. It was all a continuous cycle and it was clear, the only way to break the cycle was to deal with my past.

Likewise, Joyce Meyer openly shares her story of being sexually, emotionally, verbally, and physically abused by the most important and relevant male figure in her life – her father. She records, *"Although I appeared to function normally in society, I had multiple inward problems and complicated personality disorders...I was bitter about my past and had a chip on my shoulder, which caused me to have the attitude that everyone owed me preferential treatment. I was full of self-pity, especially if things didn't go my way. I was controlling, manipulative, fearful, insecure, and harsh. I was just plain hard to get along with and often downright obnoxious. I was judgmental, suspicious, and very negative. I experienced a lot of guilt and condemnation. I had a shame-based nature; therefore, everything I attempted was poisoned. Since I didn't like who I was, I spent many years trying to be like someone else. I'm sure you get the picture – I was quite a mess!"*[36]

Joyce Meyer credits her relationship and connection to God as the catalyst that started to transform her way of being, to free herself. She stated, *"I have changed and changed and changed. And I'm still changing! Most of those problems are completely gone, and the rest only flare up occasionally. I even look different – younger, happier, more peaceful."*[36]

THE LOVE WALK

I wholeheartedly believe that authentic love has the power to change everything.

In my quest to find peace with my past, I was blessed to have individuals cross my path who gave me a clear snapshot of what I'm calling the *love walk*.

So, what is this love walk?

I will make a bold statement here, *"Our ability to walk in love determines the quality of life we live."* Therefore, if living an amazingly extraordinary life is the goal, then mastery of this concept called love is crucial. Everything in our lives is blended into whatever level of love or apathy we choose to operate on. For me, I clearly had been operating from a state of apathy; emotionally, I was disconnected.

However, on my 35th birthday, I decided that something needed to change. It was then I really began to explore this ideology called love. During the exploration, I discovered the following major components of love: **forgiveness, acceptance, unconditionality**, and love's preserver, **vulnerability**.

FORGIVENESS

For me, **forgiveness** had to start with my dad. I had over 30 years of anger and hatred to unpack. When people hurt us, anger is usually our attempt to regain control, and unforgiveness is the result of harboring bitterness and resentment in our hearts. It is that bitterness and resentment that over time eat away at us physically, emotionally, and psychologically. Joyce Meyer stated it clearly, *"Many people ruin their health and their lives by taking the poison of bitterness, resentment and unforgiveness."*[37]

To walk in love, you must choose to live a life of forgiveness. You must accept the fact that people are not perfect; we all make mistakes, we all say and do things that hurt one another. Living a life of forgiveness means finding the space where none of it matters, where when things happen, you are able to let them go. In that space, you **choose** to forgive in every instance, whether you feel forgiveness is warranted or not. Forgiveness is the choice you must make every time, with the understanding it's for your personal benefit and not the person or people who hurt you.

Now I know from experience, this is easier said than done. In my quest to forgive my dad, I struggled with the *how-to*. I would tell myself and others that *"I forgive my dad."* However, when I thought about him, the anger and bitterness that were rooted deep inside would surface every time.

Through trial and error, I eventually discovered a process that worked for me. In general, the process of forgiveness can be complicated, but through commitment, over time it is possible. For me, forgiving my dad required a defined strategic process, and below is the four-step process I followed:

Step One: I Mentally Decided to Forgive. The very first step essentially entailed making the conscious decision to forgive myself and my dad. Self-forgiveness began with the acknowledgement and acceptance for the way I decided to act or respond to the situation.

Next, I had to decide to forgive my dad. To help in this portion of the process, I had to alter the way I interpreted the unforgiveness I was harboring. As opposed to viewing the unforgiveness as the answer, I began to view forgiveness as the answer or resolution to the problem. It wasn't that my dad deserved my forgiveness nor that I was letting him go without punishment – instead, I **chose** to release the burden I had been dragging around and forgive him for my own personal benefit. I can honestly say that I hated my dad, and that was mentally eating away at me.

Step Two: I Confronted My Dad. In order for me to move forward, confronting my dad was necessary. Now understand that I was not able to do this in person, nor did I want to. *(In fact, if you try this process, I recommend that you do not confront the offender in person unless absolutely necessary.)* Instead, I sat down and wrote a detailed letter to my dad. The objective of the letter was not to look for an apology or to necessarily ball my dad out, but to honestly express how his actions impacted me. Essentially, I used this letter to help me get the situation out of my system unto the paper. Once I completed it, I burned the letter. As the paper was being destroyed, I allowed the words on it to be destroyed in my mind and heart as well.

Step Three: I Uprooted the Negative Emotions. In this next step, I felt I needed to change the narrative. In order to do that, I needed to address the negative emotions that surfaced when I thought of my father. I instinctively knew that I needed a way to transform those negative emotions into positive ones. Now this was easier said than done.

I started with thinking about all the positives that came out of the experience. As a result of my dad, I'm extremely cautious and sensitive to the impact of addictions. Whatever I'm doing, I seek to do it in excellence – and anything done in excellence, people are willing to pay a premium price for it. My love for my mom, aunt and uncle was intensified because they did everything they could to fill the gap my dad left. I then recorded them in my journal.

Next, I chose to muster up some empathy for my dad. I know you may be thinking – *"Why on earth would you do that?"* Remember, it wasn't for the offender but 100% for me, and this did not mean that I agreed with what happened in any form or fashion. However, I wanted to try and understand possible circumstances surrounding his actions. In layman's terms, I wanted to try and walk in his shoes.

At the time, I didn't know much about my dad's upbringing or his life. Therefore, I imagined that maybe he was having a difficult time in his life. Maybe he had been hurt or abused, and as a friend once told me, *"Hurt people hurt other people."* I concluded with the following statement that I wrote in my journal: *"I understand that my father was hurt really bad at some point in his life, and he turned to drugs to help him cope with his pain. Because of this, his decision to leave our family was the best decision for him and us at that time."*

Step Four: I Prayed for My Dad. The last step in my process entailed praying for my dad. Over the years, I have learned that it is absolutely impossible to harbor anger and resentment over time when I consistently pray for someone's well-being. I also know that in the beginning, those prayers did not sound too positive. At times, all I could say was, *"God bless my dad today."* As time went on, I begin to pray for his breakthrough and deliverance...and then the prayers got longer and more authentic, until one day I looked up and the hatred, anger, bitterness, and resentment had subsided. I was able to authentically pray for him and sincerely wish him well...it was at that point where forgiveness had taken over.

Now this process may not work for everyone, but it worked for me then, and I still go back to it on occasion as needed.

ACCEPTANCE

The second major component of love that I have found is **acceptance**. Acceptance is receiving things and people as they are and as they are not, without attempting to change or protest anything. Essentially, you are **choosing** to accept people and situations at face value.

When I initially decided to forgive my dad, I told myself that I wasn't interested in having a relationship with him because I didn't want to deal with his drug addiction. And I was completely fine standing in that position. However, for me, that decision was not factoring in acceptance. I was still allowing his drug addiction to determine my response to him, as opposed to accepting him as he is and as he is not.

Now this does not mean that you have to rekindle a relationship with the individual(s) – but it does mean that you no longer hold their faults and shortcomings against them. Instead, you choose to accept that they are the way they are, period! And I encourage you to continue to pray for their deliverance, for their breakthrough – it's just your acceptance of them is not contingent on them walking in that deliverance or breakthrough.

Today, I **choose** to accept my father as he is and as he isn't. Therefore, his mess doesn't matter, it is no longer a factor and as a result, a relationship is possible.

UNCONDITIONALITY

The third major component of love that I found is **unconditionality**. Unconditionality is **choosing** to love people independent of any expectations, anticipated reciprocity, considerations, limitations, conditions, etc. You **choose** to freely love and expect nothing in return.

Several years ago, I participated in an intensive personal growth and development program. One of the techniques used in the program really shined a bright light on the causes and effects of the choices we make inside of our relationships. In general, when we **choose** to attach conditions and rights vs. wrongs to relationships, we give up our happiness, joy, peace, and freedom. At times, we can become so consumed with keeping track and ensuring the conditions or expectations are being met inside our relationships. There's a quote from *The Shack*, one of my favorite fiction books of all time that reads, *"Rights are where survivors go, so that they won't have to work out relationships."*[38] Think about this for a moment: Who wants to be in a relationship with someone and they are always wrong? But that's exactly what happens when we are always right.

However, when we **choose** to love unconditionally, we are free to just live and enjoy life – no record-keeping, no pressures – just love.

IT'S OK TO BE VULNERABLE

Vulnerability is one of those topics that people like me tend to stay far away from. Because I struggle with abandonment and rejection, the thought, the idea, the definition of the word used to terrify me:

VULNERABILITY DEFINED[39]

According to vocabulary.com, vulnerability is defined as:
- easily hurt or attacked
- susceptibility to injury or attack
- the state of being vulnerable or exposed
- state of being open to injury, or appearing as if you are

In other words, vulnerability leaves you open to the good, bad, and ugly inside relationships.

However, several years ago, I heard Brené Brown, author of *The Power of Vulnerability*, say when we are vulnerable, *"we are allowing ourselves to be deeply seen; to love with our whole heart, with no guarantees; to practice gratitude and joy; and to believe we are enough."*[40]

For me, this definition really shined a light on my insecurities. It took me back to the narrative I created as a child when my father left, I wasn't good enough for him to stay. Brown's definition challenged me to consider that my issue with vulnerability had very little to do with people abandoning, rejecting or hurting me, but everything to do with me not believing I'm good enough. Of all the great things I believe about myself, that one thing has held me hostage.

But here's the truth of the matter: When we **choose** to operate from a place of vulnerability, it completely transforms our experience inside relationships. There is an abundance of joy, happiness, creativity, belonging, connection, etc.

We just talked about forgiveness, acceptance, and unconditionality, these three live in the space of vulnerability. Not only do you become free, but you give others permission to be set free as well. It is absolutely amazing!!!

Now, is this difficult? I'm going to be transparent and, say, heck YES!!!

I have gotten to the place where I can be completely vulnerable with a select few. And even inside those relationships, there are times when I retreat and shut down because it becomes so overwhelming. Being vulnerable completely opens you up, and requires both courage and strength to stay there.

But here's the interesting part: in those instances where I shut down, the relationships suffer every time. We fall out, we don't speak for a period of time, it's uncomfortable, and sometimes, it gets flat out messy and nasty. All of which could have been prevented if I'd just allowed myself to remain open.

What I'm beginning to realize is, yes, people will let us down, our hearts may get broken and it will hurt; but it shouldn't stop us from allowing ourselves to be deeply seen, to love with our whole heart. Our focus shouldn't be on what could happen, but on practicing gratitude and joy, and to believing we are enough! It's not easy and it requires a lot of work, but the return on investment is phenomenal.

YOU HAVE A CHOICE

Did you notice the keyword that has been constant throughout this section? *(hint: it is in bold letters throughout.)* The word is choice, and its siblings, choose, chose.

You don't have to continue to bring your past into your present, nor your future. Ultimately you have the power to **choose** the trajectory of your life. In most instances, we make **decisions** and not **choices** in our lives.

Did you know that there's a difference between the two?

I learned the difference between the two in my personal growth and development training, and the difference is significant. When we **decide** something, we factor in all the considerations to make the decision. So that looks like, I love you because you provide for me, you protect and support me. Therefore, my **decision** to love you is based on all the things that you do for me. I love you, because...

On the flip side, when we **choose**, the considerations are there; however, they are **not** factored in the choice. So, choosing looks like – I love you simply because I love you. My love for you has nothing to do with how you feel about me or how you make me feel, what you do or don't do for me. I **choose** to love you because I **choose** to love you – that's it! Therefore, there is nothing you can do or say, or not do or say that's going to change my choice to love you. My love for you is not contingent on anything.

So, with that, you can choose right now to say **no more!** I choose to put the past behind; I choose to forgive and walk fully in love.

In addition, I want you to recognize that even though each of our past experiences may come with different levels of impact and severity, they have structured who we are and it's not all bad.

When I look back over what I've been through, I find that the obstacles, the hardships, trials and tribulations – they have prepared me for my assignment. Through them, my persona, my ZOG, has been strengthened and perfected.

And let me add, this is an ongoing process. You must be intentional about living life this way, which means you must remain aware of your triggers. Those situations that remind you of your past hurts can trigger an unconscious response. Trust me, it will happen; but when it does, it will be easier to catch.

Now, I realize that this might just be too much for you to tackle alone. If that's the case, I applaud you for recognizing that and I highly recommend that you do what I did and seek professional counseling.

Please get that this is critical...if you don't deal with your baggage now, it has the potential to slow you down or completely sabotage your progress.

It took me over 35 years and thousands of dollars to deal with my baggage and to get to the place where I am now. And, let me be clear, I still have triggers that catch me off guard. I, too, am still a work in progress. As I look back on it, I probably could've saved a considerable amount of time had I sought professional help earlier.

On the other hand, I didn't know or recognize what my issues were and that I needed help. There's a saying, *"When you know better, you do better."* So, now that you've read this, you can't say you didn't know and, as a result, you are now accountable. My apologies if that doesn't sit well with you. Please know that I am totally coming from a place of love. I can tell you from experience that taking on this topic right here can transform your entire life.

✐ DESTINY STARTER™ WORKBOOK

See Activity Four (4) in the *Destiny Starter™ Workbook* which is designed to analyze your current situation and help you start to work through some of it. I also recommend a number of personal growth and development programs to consider.

CHAPTER FIVE:

RENEWING YOU

Self-care is a deliberate choice to gift our self with people, places, things, events and opportunities that recharge our personal battery and promote whole health – body, mind and spirit.[41] – Laurie Bachanan, PhD

A s humans, we are three-part beings: spirit, body, and soul. We are 100% spirit; we have a soul and we live in a body. We are each responsible for the health and maintenance of all three of these.

So, what does that look like?

LET'S TALK ABOUT THE SPIRIT FIRST

Dionne van Zyl, the author of *Wired*, said, *"The human spirit is the core and eternal part of every human being."*[42] It is through our spirits that we are able to connect to God *(higher power, universe, etc.)*. Just as we nourish our bodies, nourishing our spirits is just as important.

Looking at the world today, we seem to be in a state of negativity, destruction, and pain. There are many opportunities to consume it on a daily basis via the media. It simply isn't realistic to believe that we can take all of it in, and it not have a negative impact on us in some form or fashion. Therefore, I believe having a place or space to release is essential.

With that, I want to encourage you to identify venues that help you relax and find your center daily, a couple of days a week, weekly or whatever frequency you choose. Possible avenues could be gardening, meditating, reading, axe throwing, etc. You have to find what works for you and be intentional about setting aside specific days and times to clear your mind and connect with your center. Your spirit desperately needs and deserves it.

LET'S TALK ABOUT THE BODY NEXT

Our bodies are the temples that house our spirits. That's precious cargo and we should be intentional about keeping our temples in tip-top condition.

Contrary to popular belief, it doesn't take a whole lot to take care of the body. It is a manner of being aware and cautious of what you put in your body, the consistency with which you exercise, and the frequency of medical check-ups.

It's not about fad diets or training to run a marathon. You can do those things, but they are not necessary. A healthy lifestyle should be the goal, and experts recommend the following:

- Eliminate processed foods.

- Eat more fruits and vegetables.

- Drink a minimum of 64 ounces of water.

- Replace soda with tea or carbonated water.

- Spend time journaling and/or meditating.

- Incorporate some type of workout regime – it could be as simple as walking 15-30 minutes a day.

- Get adequate sleep – typically 6-9 hours per night.

- At the bare minimum, have an annual physical.

The key here is consistency...if you find yourself fatigued, overweight, stressed-out – take stock of what you are doing on a consistent basis in reference to the areas bulleted above.

With that, what areas could you create new habits around, starting today?

Now to be transparent here, this is an ongoing battle for me. I do well for a season, and my body responds. Not only do I look great, but I feel great as well. And then, the next season, I'm eating horribly and not exercising – to which my body also responds. I gain weight, then fatigue and stress set in.

For me, it's a mind over matter play. So, when I say, *it doesn't take a whole lot to take care of the body* – I am not factoring in mindset. That's something entirely different and we will talk about the mind next.

But for now, I want to challenge you to commit to adhering to the bulleted items above for the next 90 days and see how your body responds. *Note: Always consult a physician before starting any workout regimen and change of diet.*

NOW, LET'S TALK ABOUT THE SOUL

The soul consists of your mind, will, emotions, creativity, and intellect. A huge component of soul renewal involves examining and possibly changing your attitude.

ATTITUDE DEFINED[43]

According to dictionary.com, attitude is defined as:

- Manner, disposition, feeling, position, etc., with regards to a person or thing; tendency or orientation, especially of the mind

Businessdictionary.com elevates the definition to the next level:

- A predisposition or a tendency to respond positively or negatively toward a certain idea, object, person, or situation
- Attitude influences an individual's choice of action, and responses to challenges, incentives, and rewards (*together called stimuli*).

ATTITUDE DEFINED[43]
The four major components of attitude are (1) Affective: Emotions or feelings. (2) Cognitive: Belief or opinions held consciously. (3) Conative: Inclination for action. (4) Evaluative: Positive or negative response to stimuli.

Most people have heard the statement that *your attitude determines your altitude* or simply put, your attitude is the defining factor of how high or far you can go in life. Best-selling author Zig Ziglar said it best: *"Your mental attitude and everything else about you is influenced or controlled by what goes into your mind. It's safe to say that you are what you are and where you are because of what has gone into your mind. You change what you are and where you are by changing what goes into your mind."*[44]

Holocaust survivor, neurologist, and psychiatrist, Viktor Frankl, said, *"Everything can be taken from a man but one thing: the last of human freedoms – to choose one's attitude in any given set of circumstances, to choose one's own way."*[45]

Independent of what's happening in your world, there is always one thing you can control – which encompasses your attitude – and that's your response. I once heard someone say, *"Your response is your responsibility."* Even though you can't control external factors, you can control how you respond. You don't have to live your life at the effect of the cause, you don't have to be a victim to circumstances. You do have a say; you have a choice!

As we dive deeper into renewing your soul, let's explore the following concepts:

1. Renewing the Mind

2. The Power of Words

3. The Power of Association

4. Know Your Crazy

RENEWING YOUR MIND

Getting from the point you are now to where you want to be may require you to renew your mind and change the way you think. Les Brown said, *"Change your thinking. Change your life! Your thoughts create your reality. Practice positive thinking. Act the way you want to be, and soon you will be the way you act."*[46]

Several years ago, I read a book by Dr. Ivy Hilliard entitled *Mental Toughness For Success*. In the book, Dr. Hilliard went into great detail on how the mind works. He stated, *"To have a renewed mind is to function in accordance with a new value and belief system."*[47] To understand that statement, let's look at how the mind functions.

The mind is composed of three components: the conscious, subconscious, and unconscious. The conscious mind handles *"the initial reasoning and logical thinking that is required for concentration and purposeful thinking,"* according to Hilliard.[47] The subconscious mind is the autopilot for the conscious mind. Once the conscious mind has processed the task, the subconscious mind kicks in and takes over handling that task thereafter. From that moment on, the subconscious will perform that task requiring very little conscious thought at all. The last component of the mind is the unconscious. The unconscious mind sorts, organizes, and stores all the relevant information taken in by the conscious mind. It houses our *"belief and value systems, it is the reference point by which all things are judged,"*[47] states Hilliard.

So, let me give you an example of how the three components of the mind operate. Think back to when you first learned to ride a bike. You probably had someone *(mom or dad)* holding the bike while you were pedaling. You were most likely gripping the handlebars for dear life and you were focused on not falling off the bike. Then, at some point, whoever was guiding the bike for you let go. For a moment, you didn't realize that they had let go and you were actually riding by yourself. However, as soon as you realized that your guide was no longer there - you probably hit the ground.

You were told to brush it off and get back on the bike. You got back on and tried it again and again until you reached the point where you could ride without assistance from anyone. In fact, the more you rode, the better you got. You probably even got to the point where you could ride standing up or sitting down, with your hands on or off the handlebars with little concentration.

Once the conscious mind figured out the process, the *how-to*, along with the belief that it could actually be done, the process was stored in the unconscious mind, to later be accessed by the subconscious mind. Therefore, moving forward, the subconscious mind automatically kicks in whenever you go to ride a bike. To this very day, even if you haven't ridden a bike in years, you can hop on one and move out fairly quickly.

Now, let me highlight one component of what I just said, *the belief that it could actually be done* - if you don't believe your **it** (*whatever your it is*) is possible, then none of what I just said is relevant. For example, even if you have experienced some success with your **it** in the past, if your inner voice is telling you, *you are not smart enough to do what this book is referencing, this is impossible, you will betray or outshine those you love by stepping into the plan for your life, etc.* No matter what the narrative is, the impact tends to be the same; your unconscious mind doesn't know how to process that, and therefore it doesn't. Instead, your disbelief in the possibility of it overshadows everything else.

Therefore, to renew our minds, we have to intentionally change the way we think, what we believe, and subsequently, the way we speak.

It all starts with a reprogramming of your subconscious that will eventually get stored in the unconscious mind. Remember, it is what's stored in the unconscious mind that determines what manifests on the outside.

Operating within the framework of how our minds function, I recommend a visualization technique I learned as a basketball player. Essentially, it entails you creating your own personal commercial or YouTube video that you play over and over in your mind.

During my collegiate basketball days, there was an extended period where I struggled to score a basket. I was in a *slump*, and my coach wasn't having it. In an effort to get me out of the slump, she hired a sports psychologist to work with me. During my time with him, he taught me this invaluable visualization technique. He had me close my eyes and envision myself on the court executing quick, smooth moves and scoring baskets. I created my own personal commercial, that replayed in my mind on a daily basis. Within 30 days, I was no longer in my slump. This technique worked so well; I still use it today.

Need more convincing?

Think about the world of advertising, specifically the impact of commercials that we see and hear repeatedly. Businesses pay millions of dollars to produce and display these commercials that place their products and services on our radar, in hopes of evoking action to purchase. In the *"As a Man Thinketh"* documentary, Sherri James said it best: *"The mind is powerless to resist what is suggested to it, and over time, that which is suggested to it enough, the mind eventually accepts. Advertisers know this, and they spend billions annually, because they know that the steady drip will eventually impress your mind."*[48] The return on their investment typically pays off for advertisers. And should you choose to invest your time to create and repeatedly visualize your personal commercial, it will pay off for you as well. *(See the Destiny Starter™ Workbook for more information.)*

POWER OF WORDS

Often, I am amazed at some of the things that I hear people say. I have heard parents tell their children that they are stupid, that they will never amount to anything, refer to little girls as *mama* and little boys as *lady's man*, etc.

I know you may be thinking the latter sounds innocent, right? But what about when that little girl reaches 12 years of age and she literally is a mama? Or when the little boy grows up to be a true womanizing lady's man? We can't ignore what was spoken in and over their lives. That door was opened years before the actual manifestation because of the words that were spoken, **believed**, and stored in the unconscious mind early on.

Several years ago, I shocked my friends when I decided to denounce the sorority that I had joined in college. After I had the last of three knee surgeries, I was both mentally and physically distraught. I was medically relieved from playing basketball, which was a huge component of my life. I had played the game since the age of ten and now I was left with this void that I felt needed to be filled. In my search, I was introduced to sorority life. I went through the process and I became a super sorority girl. It literally began to consume my life, just as basketball had previously done.

Now, don't get me wrong – I **loved** being in the sorority. I still treasure the knowledge I gained and more importantly, some of the relationships that developed from that sisterhood. However, as I grew stronger in my faith – the pledge that I took when I joined the sorority was bothering me. There was a constant tug between my commitment to God and the pledge I took that allowed me entry into the sorority.

Now I know that most would say that the pledge didn't really mean what it stated. However, it was those words that gave me all the rights and privileges of membership in that sorority. It was those words that justified me as a legitimate member of the organization.

I strongly believe in the power of words. I'm constantly aware of what I speak and what I allow others to speak into my life. Words really do have power; they really do mean something. Therefore, after much prayer and communication with my pastor at the time, I made the decision that I would denounce the pledge I made to the sorority. Unfortunately, that decision shattered a couple of friendships, yet it was that decision that opened the door for me to discover my *Call*. It was that decision that has allowed me the privilege of doing what it is that I am *Called* to do to fulfill my *Purpose* on the earth.

Now, am I suggesting that all Greek members go and denounce their organizations? Absolutely not! I made a tough decision that I deemed best for me and my future.

However, I am suggesting that you get an understanding of the power of your words. Essentially, be cautious of what you speak, as your tongue can clear the path to your *Purpose*, or it can build barriers to block that path. Please realize that we were designed for our words to produce results. Remember the proverb that states, *"Death and life are in the power of your tongue."*[49] So speak life and not death to your situations.

Think about your words as missiles locked into a specific target. When you speak, the missile is released into the atmosphere in route to its target – *I am healed*. Then, you open your mouth and speak against it – *this pain is killing me*.

With those words, you've just released another missile, but this new missile's target is the first missile carrying *I am healed*. It travels until it finds and blows up the first missile, essentially cancelling out your initial confession. Your new confession is that *this pain is killing you.*

Isn't that deep?

Dr. Caroline Leaf, author of *Switch on Your Brain,* says, *"We need to realize the profound impact when you say something, you need to make sure that you mean it, otherwise you can have cognitive dissonance in your brain."*[50] *SimplyPsychology* defines cognitive dissonance as *"a situation involving conflicting attitudes, beliefs or behaviors. This produces a feeling of mental discomfort leading to an alteration in one of the attitudes, beliefs or behaviors to reduce the discomfort and restore balance."*[51]

In his book, *The Law of Confession,* Bill Winston states, *"Most people have not made the connection between what they say and what they have in life...For those of us who can speak, we must learn about the law of confession and operate in it. We can have what we say! That is the power of our words."*[52]

With that being said, in addition to your commercial, I recommend that you create a personal confession or affirmation that you recite daily. I created my first confession or affirmation years ago and have adjusted it over time, but I still say or listen to a recorded version of it daily. I choose to incorporate Scriptures in mine, but you can choose whatever positive statements speak to you:

ANITA'S CONFESSION/AFFIRMATION

Thank you for making me so wonderfully complex! Your workmanship is marvelous—how well I know it. You watched me as I was being formed in utter seclusion, as I was woven together in the dark of the womb. You saw me before I was born. Every day of my life was recorded in your book. Every moment was laid out before a single day had passed. How precious are your thoughts about me, O God. They cannot be numbered! - Psalms 139:14-17 (NLT)

Father, in the name of Jesus, I thank you that I AM the seed of Abraham and his anointing of real estate, stocks and bonds is upon me. Like Abraham, I walk upright in righteousness, faith, and love. I AM obedient to Your Word and I diligently follow Your direction. I AM a virtuous woman - I AM trustworthy, I AM supportive, I AM

ANITA'S CONFESSION/AFFIRMATION

skillful and creative, I AM diligent, I AM organized, I AM always prepared, I AM 190lbs and healthy, I AM compassionate, I AM beautiful, I AM stylish, I AM powerful beyond measure, I AM secure, I AM wise, I AM nurturing, I AM deserving of praise, I AM an amazing wife with an amazing husband. I AM forgiving and refuse to hold grudges against anyone. I AM an Intercessor, Worshiper, Praiser, and Giver. I AM an Extraordinary Connector and a Transformational Leader. I AM a Best-selling Author and a Well-sought-after Speaker. I'm grateful that You have given me the power to get wealth, taught me to profit, and promised never to leave me nor forsake me. I AM the head and not the tail, above only and not beneath. I AM the lender and not the borrower. I AM a successful businesswoman with multiple streams of income. I AM like a tree planted by the rivers of water, bringing forth my fruit right now, because this is my season. I AM in the land You promised me with multiple properties, I eat without scarceness, and I lack nothing. I AM out of debt; all of my needs are met, and I have plenty put up in storehouses. I AM a blessing to all that come in contact with me. From my bank accounts I make daily transactions, participating in the establishment of Your Kingdom here on earth. Not only have you blessed me, but Your blessing has also extended to my family. Together we are leaving an inheritance for our children's children and You shall increase us more and more.

Now Father, everything that I just spoke is in alignment with Your Word and *Purpose* for my life. The Bible tells me that so shall your Word be that goes forth out of your mouth – it shall not return to you void [without producing any effect, useless], but it shall accomplish that which you please and purpose, and it shall prosper in the thing for which you sent it. You also said, no weapon formed against me shall prosper and every lying tongue that shall rise against me in judgment shall be condemned. And, last but definitely, not least, you said that you will rebuke the devourer for my sake, and he will not destroy the fruits of my ground.

I thank you and call it done, in the matchless name of Jesus Christ...Amen!

You are welcome to use my confession as a template or create your own from scratch. Once you've created it, you want to commit to reading it daily. Most mornings, I like to look in a mirror as I say my confession. If reading isn't your thing, record it on your mobile device and listen to it daily. It doesn't matter if you read or listen when you first wake up, as you're getting dressed, en route to or from work, before you go to sleep, as long as you are intentional about reading or listening to it on a consistent basis.

* * *

The simple fact here is that the mind doesn't distinguish between your dreams, visions, visual or audio messages, and real-life experiences. Therefore, repetition of both the visual and verbal exercises are vital to overriding the data stored in the unconscious mind. The more you see and speak it over time, you begin to believe it, and that eventually overrides the old belief system. Then the subconscious kicks in, to automatically bring that thing to fruition. The formula's simple — your thinking determines your beliefs, those beliefs conform your heart, out of the heart the mouth speaks, and what you speak manifests your *Destiny*.

THE POWER OF ASSOCIATION

I've always believed that it is important to be cautious concerning the people that you hang around. Deposits, both good and bad, are constantly being made amongst the people in your inner circle.

I like to use the analogy of plugging a cord into an electrical outlet. When you connect with people, you literally plug into them and they also plug into you. And just as the currents alternate when you plug into an electrical outlet, what's in you flows into them and vice versa. It is the reason a good behaving kid can be contaminated if he or she hangs around a group of bad behaving kids. The negative deposits that are being made have the potential to override the moral and value compass that exist, and bad choices are made.

Therefore, it is crucial that you surround yourself with positive, like-minded individuals who can encourage you on your journey. There is a passage in the book, *Three Feet From Gold* that has stayed with me and it reads, *"We believe that you are a direct reflection of the five people you associate with most, and your income, attitude and lifestyle is the average of those five people. If you surround yourself with leaders, you will eventually become one too. Unfortunately, it works the opposite way too."*[53]

Therefore, you want to ensure that you hang around people who have goals and are working to achieve them. These people will encourage you when needed and lift you up when you are feeling down.

I am blessed daily by the people in my inner circle. I have purposely connected with positive individuals who are smarter and make more money than me. I am like a sponge, absorbing all the information that I can from them – constantly increasing my knowledge. In addition, my inner circle is the kind that encourages me, but most importantly, corrects me when I'm wrong. You need real people like that in your life, to keep you on track.

As one of my friends once stated, *"It is important to have 'unbendable' people in your life to hold you accountable."* I am truly grateful for those in my inner circle.

KNOW YOUR CRAZY

I have a friend who wanted to divorce her husband of several years. She had reached her tipping point and decided she was done. In a conversation, she shared with me all the issues and challenges that were making her marriage unbearable. From her perspective, all the issues were on her husband – what he was and was not doing inside the marriage.

I listened attentively and when she finished, I asked, *"So inside all of that, what could you do differently?"*

Sounding extremely flustered and frustrated, she responded, *"Nothing, didn't you hear what I just said? He's the problem. He's the reason I'm so fed up, he's the reason I'm miserable. He needs to learn how to be a man, husband, and father. The way I see it, I have two choices: 1) I can choose to stay for the sake of the kids; or 2) I can choose to leave and regain my sanity." (Note: we learned previously, neither of those are choices, but they are decisions.)*

Now I'm sure you can imagine the level of steam and negative energy coming through my phone by this point. And, with that, I regretfully opted to just leave it alone. However, what I really wanted to say and should have said was the following...

You know you could choose to stay, honor the covenant you made with God and your husband, and be happy. That's the real choice that's available to you. And with making that choice, then you can figure out what you need to do on your end to make that your reality.

You see, when we allow others to make us angry, to take our peace, make us miserable, take our joy and happiness – we are giving them complete control. In every situation, we can choose our response...and it's time we take back control. It all starts with self-awareness.

Viktor Frankl simply said it this way, *"When we are no longer able to change a situation, we are challenged to change ourselves."*[45]

In addition, one thing that I found to be true is that when I show up differently inside my relationships, miraculously so do the other individual(s) in the relationship(s). The experiences inside our relationships are completely transformed, simply because I showed up differently.

With that being said, it is vital that you discover your trigger points or *hot buttons*. In other words, you must know your crazy...we all have some crazy inside of us. Once you know your crazy, then you are better positioned to put a plan in place to manage it.

Judge Lynn Toler[54] previously of *Divorce Court* said it this way, *"...the time to decide not to get angry about something is before you get angry about anything. You got to have a game plan in place for how you are going to conduct yourself, how you are going to deal with upset. And you got to know who you are, you got to dissect where you are weak. I got a list of 20 things I know that are wrong with me. I own it, I re-look at it sometimes just to make sure I'm on top of it."*

She goes on to explain how to stay on top of your crazy after you make the list...

"...you have to say to yourself, self today, just today, I'm not going to get angry. What I'm going to do is (raise your hand and say) I surrender! You surrender to your better self and then sit down. And you cannot speak until you are not angry anymore. You won't be able to do it the first couple of times, but [you will] after a while...and then at the end of the day, you got to debrief your crazy."

"Take a sheet of paper and write down the issue or situation and then write down what really happened. When you go back to read it, you will realize just how irrelevant the entire scenario was."

So, I challenge you to take time to create your list of crazies. Next, tune in to how you respond to the situations, circumstances, and challenges in your world. Then create a plan of attack...it could simply be as Judge Toler suggested, *I surrender.*

And every time one of the crazies on your list shows up...you respond in the way in which you've planned. Also, be patient with yourself and know that it will take practice. But, if you stick with it, I promise it will transform your life, and possibly the lives of those around you. *(See the Destiny Starter™ Workbook for more information.)*

DISCOVER HOW YOU OPERATE BEST

I am a huge proponent of personal assessments. I believe, they not only give you insights on your personality and how you operate best, but they help you to understand how to work best with others who may operate differently from you.

I invite you to fully discover how you operate best by exploring assessments. Keep in mind, there are no right or wrong answers for assessments. The purpose is not to judge you, but to help you get to know yourself better. I recommend the following assessments because together, they help you determine how you operate best:

DiSC®.[55] The *DiSC®* profile helps you identify your human behavior based on four styles: Dominance, Influence, Steadiness, Conscientiousness.

16 Personalities.[56] The *16 Personalities* assessment was developed using the philosophies of Carl Gustav and Katherine and Isabel Briggs (*creators of the Myers-Briggs Type Indicator*[57]). It helps you access your strengths and weaknesses to live a better life.

StrengthsFinder.[58] The *Gallup's StrengthsFinder* assessment helps people discover their unique combination of strengths. It is crucial that you know your areas of strength, so that you can focus on them. Then you hire or collaborate with people who are strong in the areas you are not. There are 34 themes or strengths in this assessment.

High5 Test.[59] The *High5* strengths test enables you to discover your strengths, which can help you become the best version of yourself and live the best version of your life. There are 20 strengths that are recurring patterns of thoughts, decisions, actions, and feelings.

Enneagram.[60] The *Riso-Hudson Enneagram Type Indicator* assessment is a personality test based on nine personality styles: reformer, helper, achiever, individualist, investigator, loyalist, enthusiast, challenger, and peacemaker.

VIA Character Strengths Survey.[61] The *VIA* classification of character strengths and virtues are the positive parts of your personality that impact how you think, feel, and behave. Character strengths are different than your other personal strengths, such as your unique skills, talents, interests, and resources, because they reflect the "real" you — who you are at your core.

The Four Tendencies Quiz.[62] The *Four Tendencies Quiz* was developed by best-selling author, Gretchen Rubin, to help you determine how you respond to both outer and inner expectations. Your response to those expectations will align with one or a combination of the four tendencies: Upholder, Obliger, Rebel, or Questioner.

* * *

At the end of the day, when it's all said and done, you want to be the best, authentic you. Although we are in a world consumed with selfies and sharing our entire lives on social media...in most instances, we don't allow the world to see the real us. We tend to put on this mask for the world to see...our representative is front and center. As a result, very few people have the privilege of experiencing the real us. In fact, we may have even forgotten or lost who we really are.

✎ DESTINY STARTER™ WORKBOOK

See Activity Five (5) in the *Destiny Starter™ Workbook* to:
1. Develop your visualization regimen and create your personal commercial.
2. Create your daily affirmation.
3. Determine and record your crazy, along with the response you will take each time it shows up. (*I know this exercise is weird, but it can be highly effective if you do it.*)
4. Access direct links for all the assessments, including some **Free** options.

As we conclude *Part One: Let's Talk About You*, I really want to stress the importance of taking stock of the emotional baggage you may be carrying and working to overcome it. If not, please understand that it has the potential to hinder your progress as you pursue the *Call* on your life. It's important, extremely important!

Also, don't use working on yourself as an excuse for not fulfilling the *Call*. It is possible to work on them at the same time.

Now, let's move on to *Part Two: Now, Let's Talk About Your Vision.*

WHAT'S YOUR GO-TO?

I am a former player and fan of tennis, and one weekend I was watching the *U.S. Open Finals*. In the final game, Serena Williams competed against Australia's Samantha Stosur. Now understand that Stosur is an excellent tennis player; however, Williams is arguably better. At the time of this game, Williams' statistics were as follows: 40% of Williams' serves are not returned, meaning that her opponent has a 60% chance of hitting and returning any serve that Serena makes. Then despite the percentage of serves that are successfully returned to her, she still wins 80% of all the sets that she serves. Therefore, her opponent has only a 20% chance of even winning the match if Williams serves. Talk about the odds being stacked against you!

Although Serena was arguably the better, more experienced athlete, she lost the game. She lost the game because Stosur not only showed up, but she showed up with her "A" game. As opposed to Williams who was only physically present – her body was there and that was it.

So, it got me thinking about the simple truths that pertain to the games that we all are playing in life. Independent of whether you are playing the school game, the corporate America game, the business professional game, the athletic game, or the entrepreneurial game, these basic truths remain the same. In order to win the game you are playing:

1. You must get on the court. Stop making excuses and rewrite the story with you physically on the court.

2. Not only must you physically get on the court, but you must mentally show up to play your game, meaning you must condition your mind for the game.

3. Find your go-to and perfect it. For Serena Williams, her *"go-to"* is her amazing ability to hit that deadly serve. Because she has perfected that part of her game, any and every time she physically and mentally gets on the court – she can always go to her serve to guarantee a win majority (~80%) of the time!

So, I encourage you to take the time to plan, prepare, and perfect your *"go-to"* for the game you are playing in your life.

– Anita "AC" Clinton

Part Two:

Now, Let's Talk About Your Vision

CHAPTER SIX:

WHAT'S THE VISION?

If you are working on something exciting that you really care about, you don't have to be pushed. The Vision pulls you.[63] *– Steve Jobs*

I n the first marker of this book, you defined your *Zone of Greatness* (ZOG), or that thing that you are passionate about, have a skill set to do it, and it serves others. Here, we will take that to the next level.

We will marry your ZOG with a change you want to see in the world or your vision for the world.

As defined by *Merriam-Webster*, *"Vision is a thought, concept or object, formed by the imagination."*[64] The *New Oxford American Dictionary* says, *"Vision is the ability to think about or plan the future with imagination or wisdom; a mental image of what the future will or could be like."*[65]

Now that's awesome!!!

When you think about your passion, what do you see? How do you envision the world transforming when you step into your ZOG? If you have young children, nieces, nephews, cousins, etc. – what do you want the world to look like when they become adults?

In other words, *what is the change you want to see in the world?* You may or may not be able to answer that right now, but hold on, we will get you there...

LAYING THE FOUNDATION

Several years ago, I attended a conference where Tudor Bismark was speaking on this concept he called, *The Golden Age.*[66] He defined the Golden Age as the season where the right people are doing the right thing. He spoke extensively about four distinct classes of people in the world:

Class 1: Wrong People Doing the Wrong Things. An example of this would be the individuals fueling the corruption and greed that we've seen on Wall Street and the banking industry. They are blatantly doing things that negatively impact our society.

Class 2: Wrong People Doing the Right Things. This will be those leaders doing things that positively impact society (*i.e. providing jobs, manufacturing goods, etc.*), but using the proceeds to finance agendas that hurt, as opposed to helping the masses.

Class 3: Right People Doing the Wrong Things. Those who are working for others, using their talents and gifts for the benefit of someone else's vision that's not serving the masses. When instead, they should be using them to advance their own visions or dreams and positively changing our world.

Class 4: Right People Doing the Right Things. Here you have the right people stepping up and into that which they were created to do, positively impacting lives, and transforming the world in which we live.

WHAT'S YOUR LANE?

Now is the time for the right people to find their lane, and start doing the right thing. When talking about the *Call* on our lives, we each have a lane, environment, element in which our ZOG operates best. We are *Called* to impact and influence the *7 Mountains of Culture*[67] that shape the culture of every community, region, and nation. As referenced by Lance Wallnau,[68] *whoever dominates these 7 mountains can literally shape the agendas that form nations:*

BUSINESS   EDUCATION   ENTERTAINMENT   FAMILY   GOVERNMENT   MEDIA   RELIGION

As you fulfill the *Call* on your life, you will operate in at least one of these mountains. We dig deeper into this in the *Destiny Starter™ Digital Course* and *Live Trainings*.

Within your mountain(s), you will most likely operate inside a **business, ministry, movement, cause,** or **career**. Now, your *Call* can span across two or more of these, but at least one will be a fit.

BUSINESS, MINISTRY, MOVEMENT, CAUSE, OR CAREER

Business:

The activity of making, buying, selling goods, or providing services or programs that positively impact society in exchange for money. A business can be independent (*solopreneur, entrepreneur, parallel-preneur, small business, etc.*), a joint venture, a franchise, etc. in either the non-profit or for-profit sectors, typically in the marketplace.

Ministry:

The act of meeting the needs of society spiritually, emotionally, mentally, physically, or financially. Ministry can occur inside a church, missions, a non-profit or the marketplace. (*Note: Because ministries require an ongoing supply of capital to effectively function, there is often a business side of ministry.*)

Movement:

The act or process of moving people or things from one place or position to another. A movement can be independent or a component of an existing organization (*i.e., Civil Rights Movement, Me Too Movement, Occupy Wall Street Movement*).

Cause:

Something or someone that produces an effect, result, condition or makes something happen or exist. Causes can take place independently or inside a profession, small business, corporation, or ministry. The perfect example is the *Innocence Project*[69] which is committed to exonerating those who have been wrongfully convicted. The project started as a cause by Professor Barry Scheck working at the *Benjamin N. Cardozo School of Law*.

Career:

A career is a professional journey where individuals continually advance until they arrive at a specific destination. It will usually entail a salary, with benefits and can expand across different organizations at different times throughout the journey. In addition, the activity of making, buying, selling goods, or providing services or programs could also occur inside an existing organization known as intrapreneurship. We discuss this in greater detail below...

With that being said, your *Call* could very well be manifested inside your own business or inside of working in or for someone else's business. I understand that not everyone is meant to be an entrepreneur or business owner; it is possible to fulfill the *Call* inside your career, working as an employee or somewhere in between.

For example, through this process, you may discover that you are an intrapreneur. Intrapreneurs are individuals who use their creativity, innovation and ZOG inside the company they work for. As defined by Investopedia, *"an intrapreneurship is a system which allows an employee to act like an entrepreneur within an organization... Employees use their entrepreneurial skills for the benefit of both the company and the employee. It gives employees the freedom to experiment, as well as the potential for growth within an organization."*[70]

Maybe you have a new idea or concept that will improve your company's processes and procedures, or you have a new idea for a product or service that will enhance those already being offered. Essentially, intrapreneurship allows employees to have somewhat of an entrepreneur-ish experience inside their employment.

Let me give you an example. Years ago, I worked for this company that paid me well, and I loved what I did because I got to fix problems. Inside my department, however, the employee morale was horrific.

Here I was, a couple of years out of college, I had landed the perfect job, and had stepped into an environment where these real grown folks were draining all my energy with their negativity. I wasn't used to this type of environment, and being the fixer that I am, I decided to come up with a solution that I called *T.E.A.M.2000 (Together Everyone Achieves More in 2000)*

I took the idea to a couple of co-workers who were feeling my pain. Together, we tweaked it and presented it to our direct manager, who then scheduled a meeting for us to present it to the Director of our division.

The Director loved it, we implemented the plan with the full support of management, and it worked. It was an extremely simple acknowledgement and reward concept that was impactful for both our department and me because it put me on upper management's radar. So, when the next round or opportunities for promotions came, you better believe my name was in the hat; in fact, I got promoted two (2) times within a 4-year period.

Yes, I was good at my job which helped warrant the promotions, but *T.E.A.M.2000* opened the doors.

Another example of intrapreneurship would be the creation of *Sony's Playstation*. It has been said that *Sony* employee, Ken Kutaragi, spent hours trying to make his daughter's *Nintendo* console more powerful and user-friendly. As a result of his intrapreneurial ideas and effort came the *Sony Playstation*.

According to Statista.com, *"Sony's PlayStation line of gaming consoles ranks as one of the most successful console brands of all time – five of its products ranking among the top ten highest selling consoles in history. The PlayStation 2 ranks at the top of this list with over 157 million units sold, while the more recent PS4 ranks sixth, generating an additional 92 million unit sales throughout its lifetime. The online entertainment network associated with the consoles is called the PlayStation Network, and as of March 2019 had around 94 million active users."*[71]

As you can see, intrapreneurship can be extremely impactful, and allows you the opportunity to explore your creative and innovative ideas inside the comfort of receiving a steady paycheck. On the flipside, you may not financially benefit from the profits generated by the development and sale of your ideas, because it is considered *work for hire*.

If intrapreneurship is not for you, maybe there's a movement or cause within you that could align with your employer's purpose, or even be launched as a new division within the company that you manage or work in.

Or your ZOG could be in perfect alignment with your employer's mission and vision, and you do your part to serve and impact through the organization.

Or better yet, maybe your *Calling* takes you into the business sector *(either for profit, non-profit or both)*.

My point is that there is no cookie-cutter way for you to fulfill your *Call*, but only possibilities for you to define your lane and create your path, however you choose.

Now take a moment and ponder the following questions:

1. Does your ZOG align best with a business, ministry, movement, cause, career, or a combination of these?

2. Does it align with your job or what you are currently doing?

The first question is simply a reference to help you see where you fit.

The second question, however, confirms whether or not your current position or job is right for you. Now, if you discover the answer is no, **don't go and quit your job tomorrow**. Chill out, you need a plan for that, and we will discuss that plan later in the book.

For now, let's construct the framing for your *Call*.

CONSTRUCT THE FRAMING

The framing for your *Calling* is constructed by defining the following six (6) variables: *Why, Who, What, How, Where,* and *When*. On the following pages, we will walk you through these variables as it relates to your ZOG. Keep in mind that these variables can apply to both employer and employee status – either way – you are assessing each based on your individual ZOG.

NUMBER ONE: WHY

First you want to think through your *Why*. It is essentially your response to a challenge or pain that you see in the world. It is the *Why* that keeps you connected, that keeps you motivated and inspired to keep moving forward no matter what comes your way.

As referenced earlier in the book, inside of you is the solution or answer to at least one of the challenges that exist today. That means the **entire world** is waiting on you and your *Greatness* to show up.

With that in mind, what's that primary thing that bothers you in or with today's society? It's the thing that really gets under your skin.

I believe the thing that bothers you the most, and in some way aligns with your ZOG, is the very thing you are the answer for. You exist to provide a solution to that problem. Your contribution in that area positively impacts other living beings, and therein lies your *Call*. In addition, the opposite of that builds the makeup of your vision.

Let me give you an example...years ago I was driving down *Cicero Avenue*, one of the most dangerous streets on the west side of *Chicago, IL*. In an attempt to bypass rush hour traffic, I ended up on this street and was looking for the fastest route off it, when I found myself frustrated behind an eighteen-wheeler slowly braking.

Adding to my frustration, I was forced to brake as the driver slowly started to pull over. I went around with my face frowned and saying a couple of choice words! Once I had fully cleared the truck, looking in the rearview mirror, I was impelled to pull over a couple of yards in front of the truck to watch what was happening.

On the sidewalk was a lady of the evening – I call her Trina – that had caught the driver's attention. I watched in tears as Trina sadly made her way to the passenger's door to speak with the driver. As she got closer, she adjusted the expression on her face, and I can only imagine how the conversation went.

At this point, the tears were streaming down my face, and I wanted to exit my car and go after Trina. I thought, there must be a better way...I refused then and now, to believe that women dream of and choose prostitution as their contribution to society. No one will ever convince me of that! And in that moment, as I searched my brain for an alternative for Trina, I had nothing.

As I watched Trina step up into the truck, I thought about all the people who work jobs that they hate or despise because they can't see another way, and it pays the bills.

There has to be a better way; there must be an alternative.

That thing bothered me so much that I created the alternative – *Be Great Global*. It is the answer to the pain that I saw in Trina's eyes on *Cicero Avenue* years ago.

Today, I want to see the masses creating joy-filled strategies to both making a living and making a life. *I believe that when people connect to and step into their purpose, it not only changes their lives, but it transforms the experience we all have on earth.* Simply put, the world becomes a better place when people are actively doing what they were created to do. We all are better for it!!! This is my *Why*.

Just as there was a pain that I felt obligated to address, you have at least one also. And like mine, it is your *Why*.

NUMBER TWO: WHO

Next, you want to think about your *Who*. Here you will answer the following questions: Who is your target audience? Who do you want to work with? Who will benefit from your ZOG? This will be your *Who*.

Looking at the generational breakdown and demographic elements below, think about the characteristics of the group(s) that you feel impelled to work with:

GENERATIONAL BREAKDOWN

Traditionalists	Baby Boomers	Generation X
(1900-1945) – 70+	(1946-1964) – 51-69	(1965-1980) – 35-50

Millennials	Boomlets
(1981-2000) – 15-34	(2000+) – 14 & under

In addition, think about other characteristics for your target audience, like gender, income, marital status, ethnicity, educational attainment, occupation, etc. You want to narrow down your target audience as much as possible.

As an entrepreneur, what you have to offer may be for everyone, but for planning and marketing purposes, your target audience **should not be everyone!** This group will help you determine how you market, where you market and what products, services, or programs you market. It's a lot easier to consider a specific group-type when planning and developing products.

Let me give you an example. Years ago, I was told at that time, *Target (the big box store)* had narrowed their target audience down to caucasian women with a household income of $100,000 or more. Does that mean that a black woman with a $60,000 household income couldn't shop at *Target*? No! It just meant that when *Target* was thinking about the types of products to put on the shelves, their marketing campaigns, etc...they primarily had the caucasian woman with a household income of $100,000 or more in mind. Your target audience should be just as specific...for the same reasons.

As an employee or intrapreneur, your target audience could be two-fold: 1) your target employer, and 2) the group you feel compelled to work with, which should align with your employer's target audience. If it doesn't align, maybe this presents an opportunity for you to propose a new product, service, or program that benefits your defined target audience within the organization. Or consider exploring employment at other organizations that would be a better fit for your *Who*.

Create Your Avatar

Note: This next section may or may not be relevant if you are an employee or intrapreneur, but I recommend that you go through this section and give it a try.

Based on the target audience defined, I want you to create an avatar for your audience. It will represent your ideal clients, customers, supporters, or followers. As defined by *Merriam-Webster*, an avatar is *"someone who represents a type of person, and idea or a quality."*[72] Hubspot defined an avatar as *"a fictional character that represents your ideal prospect. When complete, it will help you understand the motivating beliefs, fears and secret desires that influence your customer's buying decisions."*[73]

So here, I want you to really think about who he, she or it is, what they are currently doing, what they like and don't like, what their struggles or pain points are, what's important to them, etc. Remember, this is your ideal client, customer, supporter, or follower. (*Note: Even if you are Called to work with other living beings like animals, plants, etc., your avatar may still be a human being who owns and cares for the living being you are targeting.*)

Below you will find brief descriptions of my male and female avatars for *Be Great Global.* (*Note: Depending on your target audience, you may not have both a male and female avatar.*)

BGG AVATARS

Female Avatar – Meet Michelle:

Michelle is a smart and resourceful woman. She loves people and is willing to help anyone, and many times, people have taken advantage of her giving and kind heart. She has a healthy balance between intellect and common sense.

She is engaged in transformation or inner development work, and she is a knowledge seeker. She is educated and passionate about making a difference in the world. She is a fashionable go-getter and takes pleasure in being well put together. She dines out, goes to the theatre, movies, and other events. She is worried about not being present for her family and, therefore, appears to have lost herself inside her career and family life.

She has a decent paying job but wants more. She knows there is more to her life...she knows there is something else she should be doing, but she's just not sure what it is. As a result, she has desperately been seeking the *Purpose* for her life.

Male Avatar – Meet Michael:

Michael is a mighty man. Although he is not perfect, his morals and values are important to him.

He is educated and passionate about making a difference in the world. He is a fashionable go-getter and takes pleasure in being well put together. He is concerned about providing for his family and desperately wishes he had more time to enjoy life.

He is currently working a job that pays the bills but is not fulfilling. He longs for something else; he just doesn't know what that something else is...but knows there should be more to his life. As a result, he has desperately been seeking the *Purpose* for his life.

Name Your Tribe

In his book, *Tribes*, Seth Godin defines tribes as *"any group of people, large or small who are connected to one another, a leader and an idea."*[74] At the end of the day, people want to feel like they belong, like they are connected to something that's bigger than them.

So, as you are building, the ultimate goal here is for your target audience to become a part of your tribe. Therefore, it may be beneficial to define how you will reference that audience. Are they customers, clients, followers, partners, supporters, or are they given a specific name? For example, thought leader and health expert, Chalene Johnson, calls her tribe *lifers*. I call my tribe, the *BG (Be Great) Squad*.

NUMBER THREE: WHAT

Now, let's move on to your *What*. It is synonymous with your vision. Here you will answer the following questions: What can your target audience expect from you? What can your target audience come to you for? What challenge(s) or pain(s) are you solving?

Keep in mind, this is different from *How* you do *What* you do. Your *What* will take into consideration your target audience and *What* you help them do or overcome, to improve their life and help them make a difference somehow in the world.

My *What* is as follows: *I help intrapreneurs and entrepreneurs find happiness, fulfillment, and money, doing work they actually love.* As you can see, my *What* and my ZOG *Statement* are the same.

SWOT Analysis

Next, we will focus on your *SWOT Analysis*, where we define your strengths, weaknesses, opportunities & threats. Independent of whether you are an employer or employee, the focus of this *SWOT* is centered around *What* you do. This analysis will help you view your *What* from different perspectives, identify areas of personal and professional development or operational improvement, tackle, or bypass risks, discover emerging opportunities and more:

BGG SWOT ANALYSIS

	HELPFUL (FOR YOUR OBJECTIVE)	HARMFUL (FOR YOUR OBJECTIVE)
INTERNAL	**Strengths** • Awesome, easy to understand concept • Committed and motivated leader • Ability, confidence & expertise to pull this off • Ability to create or use strategic alliances • Great timing – this is the season	**Weaknesses** • Organization is new and unknown • Limited staff • Limited financial resources • Launching too much, too soon
EXTERNAL	**Opportunities** • Create an environment where the tribe is an intricate part of the team who support and promote the *Be Great* brand • To inspire 1 billion dreamers to fulfill the *Call* on their lives • More people are seeking alternatives. People want to be a part of something bigger and greater than themselves	**Threats** • Saturation in podcasting space • Keeping up with technology • Oversaturated markets

Strengths. Think about your internal strong suits or strong variables that will work in your favor. They are the things that will give you advantages over others. Essentially, your strengths are internal qualities that will be helpful for you inside your *Call*.

Weaknesses. Here you want to think about your internal areas of weaknesses. What are those things you could probably improve on, that you should stay away from, or are limitations or barriers that exist for you? Your weaknesses are internal variables that could be harmful. Therefore, if necessary, seek outside assistance to help you combat or handle these when needed.

Opportunities. These fall in the external category. What are the external factors or variables that will work in your favor? Are there trends, patterns, changes, etc. that are coming or occurring that will benefit you? Opportunities are external factors that could be helpful for your *Call*.

Threats. These also land in the external category. What are the external factors or variables that could possibly hinder or create a barrier for you? Threats are those external factors which are out of your control that could be harmful to your *Call*.

NUMBER FOUR: HOW

The *How* is what tends to trip people up. It is often confused with the *What*, and although the *How* and *What* are vastly different, they dance very well together. In this section, you want to answer the following questions: How do you share and deliver your message, product, service, or program to your target audience? How does what you do answer their challenge(s) or solve their pain(s)?

It's essentially *How* you do *What* you do. To state it another way, your How is your assignment.

Think back to your ZOG – do you sing, write, dance, teach, inspire, motivate, create websites, knit, etc.? It's essentially the activity you do inside your *Call*. Think about the title you would most likely use to describe who you are to your audience: singer, writer, dancer, coach, speaker, product manufacturer, project manager, publisher, graphic designer, lawyer, etc.

Note: it is possible for your How to be multifaceted, and it can change several times over time. For instance, my *How* initially entailed brand development, graphic and website design. Today, I'm focused more on speaking, teaching, and writing. Remember, your *Call* remains pretty constant over your lifetime. However, your assignment or *How* you fulfill the *Call* may change many times throughout your lifetime.

Your How as An Employee

As an employee or intrapreneur, your *How* will most likely align with your job description, if you are in the right position. If you are in the wrong position, what's your perfect job or position? To help you identify that, consider what products, services, or programs your employer offers, and how you can use your ZOG to best assist – this is the position you should seek. If you can't find a connection, it may be time that you consider exploring other employment opportunities that better align. These opportunities can be within the organization that you already work for or not.

We will help you break this down in greater detail in the next chapter, *Start Writing the Plan*.

Your How as An Entrepreneur or Small Business Owner

As an entrepreneur or small business owner, you have the following to consider:

Products, Services, Programs. You will build your products, services, or programs needed to fulfill your vision under the *How*. For instance, if you are consulting or coaching, you want to create the programs you will offer. It could look something like:

- **Individual Coaching.** *90-Day Challenge* will include a 30-minute assessment, 6: 1-hour phone sessions *(2 per month)*, and a personality test.

- **Group Coaching.** *90-Day Mastermind* will include weekly 1-hour conference calls, goal setting worksheet, and an accountability forum.

In addition, when developing your products, services, or programs, be sure to consider necessary intellectual property or proprietary rights:

- **Patents.**[75] The *United States Patent and Trademark Office (USPTO)* is the Federal agency that grants U.S. patents and registers trademarks. A patent is an intellectual property right granted by *USPTO "to exclude others from making, using, offering for sale, or selling the invention throughout the U.S. or importing the invention into the U.S."* for a limited time in exchange for public disclosure of the invention when the patent is granted. There are three (3) types of patents:

  - *Utility Patents* may be granted to anyone who invents or discovers any new and useful process, machine, article of manufacture, or composition or matter, or any new and useful improvement thereof.

  - *Design Patents* may be granted to anyone who invents a new, original, and ornamental design for an article of manufacture.

  - *Plant Patents* may be granted to anyone who invents or discovers and asexually reproduces any distinct and new variety of plant.

- **Trademarks & Service Marks.**[75] The term *trademark* is often used to refer to both trademarks and service marks. A trademark is a word, phrase, symbol or design, or a combination thereof, that identifies and distinguishes the source of the goods of one party from those of another. A service mark identifies and distinguishes the source of a service rather than goods.

- **Copyrights.**[76] Copyright is a form of protection provided by the laws of the United States to the authors of original work of authorship, including literary, dramatic, musical, architectural, cartographic, choreographic, pantomimic, pictorial, graphic, sculptural and audiovisual creations. Copyright protection does not extend to any idea, procedure, process, slogan, principle, or discovery. (Note: *Your work is automatically protected when you first create it. Officially registering a copyright gives you the opportunity to seek statutory damages and attorney fees in the event of litigation.*)

NUMBER FIVE: WHERE

As an entrepreneur or business owner, you want to define where your business, ministry, movement, or cause is located. Are you online, offline, or both? Will you have a brick-and-mortar location? Think about your target audience, where do they hang out – locations or geographic areas, online communities, etc.? At the end of the day, you want to be *Where* they are.

However, as an employee or intrapreneur, your *Where* will be determined by your employer's locale, or approved working sites.

NUMBER SIX: WHEN

If you discover that what you are currently doing isn't in alignment with your ZOG, you want to define *When* you see yourself getting started. Here I want you to pick a firm date that you will launch your business, ministry, movement, cause, or job search. I'm talking about a specific month, day, and year. From there, you will reverse engineer or work backwards to develop a plan of action to ensure you meet that launch date.

Although exceedingly small, this piece is important. For some, it may be as easy as picking a date on your calendar, then reverse engineering your steps to ensure you are ready.

For others, you may already be balancing several things in your life. So, answering the *When* question will take much more consideration. The bottom line is that you must be willing to allocate time to work on your *Call*.

Therefore, the questions become: When can you devote time during the week to work on this? What are you willing to sacrifice to get it done?

Let's be clear, you will have to sacrifice something: sleep, time with family and friends, extra-curricular activities, etc. This doesn't necessarily mean that you completely eliminate these things, but that you spend less time doing some of them to free up time to work on your *Vision*. Once you determine your date, take a minute, and add it to your calendar.

* * *

Your vision is the foundation of the *Call*. You must be intentional about building that foundation in the very beginning because it will support everything you build thereafter. If the foundation is weak, it won't be strong enough to handle the pressure and the storms ahead. And take it from me, it's not a matter of if the pressure and storms come, but when they come. Therefore, you want to ensure that the vision is solid and that you share it with others every chance you get.

✎ DESTINY STARTER™ WORKBOOK

See Activity Six (6) in the *Destiny Starter™ Workbook* to map out your vision:

1. Define the underlying reason for your *Call*.
2. Define your target audience.
3. Define what your target audience can expect from you.
4. Define how you will share and deliver what you offer.
5. Define where your venture will be located (*if applicable*).
6. Define when you will get started.

CHAPTER SEVEN:

START WRITING THE PLAN

Remember: Most people fail, not because they lack talent, money, or opportunity; they fail because they never really planned to succeed. Plan your future because you have to live there![77] – Robert H. Schuller

Several years ago, I was standing on the 14th floor in one of the tallest buildings in downtown *Milwaukee*. From that position, I had an unobstructed view of the city, and for miles, I could clearly see the sheer beauty in the grass, flowers, and trees. In addition, there was a yellow highway leading out of the area that had been beautifully constructed with various turns and curves. There was also real estate everywhere I looked. I have always been fascinated with architecture, and more recently had begun to appreciate the intricate details and perfection inside of nature. So, as I stood there in awe, looking at the collective beautiful work between nature and man, I begin to ponder, *what should I be creating? How do I do that which I believe I've been Called to do?*

In that moment, I closed my eyes and I could see a huge white blank canvas with a variety of paint brushes and buckets full of various colors of paint. Then I heard the words, *here's the canvas, create what you want! The vision and provision have already been provided, it's your job to create a plan and take action.*

For me, the vision entailed seeing masses of people doing work that they are passionate about, work that transforms the experience we all have in the world. However, there are at least one of three barriers stopping them:

1. Not knowing what they were created to do

2. Not knowing how to do what they are created to do

3. The overwhelming and stifling fear around doing what they were created to do alone

Armed with that information, I set out to do exactly what I'm instructing you to do in this section of the book – **create a plan.**

As an entrepreneur, I've been conditioned to understand the importance of planning. We have all heard the phrase, *if you fail to plan, [by default] you plan to fail.* Although we are already equipped with exactly what we need to walk in our *Call,* some type of training and preparation may still be necessary. There may be stages that you go through to get to the place of solace that represents your *Purpose,* but it is possible to get there and live your best life.

In order to get there, you need a plan, and it will vary depending on whether you are working for someone else, for yourself or both.

WORKING FOR SOMEONE ELSE

If your *Call* entails working for someone else, keep reading below. If not, skip this section and go to the next section entitled, *"Working for Yourself."*

As I mentioned previously, I understand that not everyone is *Called* to start a business, and some people will fulfill the *Call* inside of their career as an employee. Therefore, this section will focus on helping you gather the necessary information to complete your career plan as it relates to your *Call.*

In order to do that, you must know your destination – *where are you going?* Here we will circle back to your *How* from the previous chapter – *what's the title you defined? What is your perfect job?*

With your perfect job in mind, you want to begin: researching job requirements and responsibilities, determining your preparation needs, and defining your career goals.

CORE CAREER ELEMENTS

Research Job Requirements & Responsibilities

Based on the specific job position of interest, you want to research the job requirements and responsibilities for that position. *(See the template in the Destiny Starter™ Workbook.)* You will use the results of this research to help you complete the next section...

Determine Your Preparation Needs

In this section, you want to figure out what preparation is needed for your perfect job. In *Chapter 2*, we already discussed training and educational needs. Here you want to consider other needs like:

Identify Internal Opportunities. If you are currently working for an organization, what opportunities exist there that align with your ZOG? Or what opportunities can be created that align with your ZOG?

Find a Mentor or Two. As defined by dictionary.com, *"a mentor is the main person you rely on to give you advice and guidance, especially in your career."*[78] Many successful people credit their success to having a mentor. A good mentor has been where you want to go, knows where the pit holes are located, understands what it takes to get there, and can be an invaluable guide to you. Therefore, you want to consider identifying individuals inside your organization or other organizations that are doing or have done what you want to do. Once you have identified potential mentors, reach out and ask them if they would mentor you. They will mostly likely want to know your story and expectations. In addition, consider what you have to offer them. In fact, in your first meeting I suggest you inquire what you can do for them. Overall, always be prepared when you meet with them, and don't waste their time.

Interview Preparation. Coming from the belief that practice makes perfect, I want to encourage you to practice, practice, practice interviewing. You can start with searching the internet for practice interview questions. Once you have compiled a list of questions, you want to take the time to think through and practice your responses.

In addition to practicing, you want to start thinking about what attire you will wear. Pull it out and try it on to ensure that it fits and looks great. During this process, you may find that you need to do a wardrobe upgrade. If that's the case, it's time to go shopping.

Setting Up Alerts. There are many advantages in the digital world in which we live, and one of those advantages are *alerts*. Alerts monitor and notify you about new mentions on the internet around specific keywords you identify. You set up keywords, topics that hit anywhere on the web that you would like to be notified about. For instance, I have alerts set up for my name, therefore anytime my name appears in newspaper articles, forums, blogs, twitter, etc., I receive a notification. I also have alerts set up for *Call for Speakers* – this alert has been great with providing me an overview of what speaking opportunities are coming up.

You can do the same and set up alerts for specific open positions in your geographical area *(if applicable)*. There are two (2) monitoring services that I recommend: *Google Alerts* and *Talkwalker Alerts*. *(See the Destiny Starter™ Workbook for more information.)*

Define Your Career Goals

Based on a research study done by Professor Gail Matthews, PhD, *"We are 43% more likely to achieve our goals if we write them down."*[79]

With your ZOG destination in mind, begin to write down the possible avenues you will take to get there and record them. You want to define both short-term *(12 months)* and long-term goals *(5-10 years)*. In addition, these goals should be S.M.A.R.T.:

Specific. Clearly define the goal, including actual numbers *(if applicable)* for what you want to accomplish.

Measurable. You want to be able to track the goal, to ensure that it is accomplished.

Attainable. The goal should be realistic, something that you can accomplish with the time, resources, and effort put into it.

Relevant. The goal is connected to or appropriate for your venture.

Time-Bound. Designate a specific timeframe to achieve the goal.

An example S.M.A.R.T. career goal is secure a promotion to a project management role within 12 months with my current employer or at another organization. It is **specific** *(promotion to a project management role with my current employer or at another organization)*; **measurable** *(new position)*; **attainable** *(definitely doable with effort in the designated timeframe)*; **relevant** *(this role should be in perfect alignment with your ZOG)*; and **time-bound** *(the next 12-months)*.

WORKING FOR YOURSELF

If your plan is to fulfill your *Call* through starting a business *(including both non-profit and for-profit)*, then this section is for you. You will want to give the following some consideration:

CORE ORGANIZATIONAL ELEMENTS

Organizational Structures

Depending on the organizational model you choose, it might be necessary to register a separate business entity. There are a variety of structures, depending on your unique situation:

Sole Proprietorship. A sole proprietorship is by far the simplest business structure to create. It is an unincorporated business with one proprietor or owner who is personally responsible for all debts incurred. For tax purposes and identity protection, as opposed to using the proprietor's social security number, the sole proprietor can apply for a separate *Employer Identification Number (EIN)*. Although the proprietor can use the *EIN*, all business profits and losses pass through the proprietor's personal tax returns. Some examples of sole proprietorships are barbers, beauticians, massage therapists, home-based and online companies, handymen, consultants, and freelancers.

Partnership. Partnerships are formed between two or more people who embark on a trade or business. Each partner contributes money, property, labor, or skill, in return for a share in the profits and losses of the business. There are three types of partnerships:

- *General Partnerships* consist of general partners investing in the business, taking part in running it and sharing in its profits. Each general partner is fully liable for any debts that the partnership may have.

- *Limited Partnerships* consist of limited partners who are not permitted to participate in the day-to-day running of the business. Their debt is limited to the amount of their initial investment.

- *Limited Liability Partnership (LLP)* is a form of ownership in which all the partners receive limited liability protection. An *LLP* is similar to a general partnership in that all the partners can take an active role in managing the day-to-day affairs of the business. In a nutshell, it is a hybrid between a general partnership and a corporation.

A partnership must file an annual information return to report the income, deductions, gains, losses, etc., from its operations, but it does not pay income tax. Instead, it "passes through" any profits or losses to its partners. Each partner includes his or her share of the partnership's income or loss on his or her personal tax return. Some examples of partnerships are lawyers, accountants, architects, and investors.

Limited Liability Company (LLC). A limited liability company is a business structure allowed by state statute. *LLCs* are popular because, like a corporation, owners have limited personal liability for the debts and actions of the *LLC*. Other features of *LLCs* are more like a partnership, providing management flexibility and the benefit of pass-through taxation.

Owners of an *LLC* are called members. Since most states do not restrict ownership, members may include individuals, corporations, other *LLCs*, and foreign entities. There is no maximum number of members. Most states also permit "single member" *LLCs*, those having only one owner.

The federal government does not recognize an *LLC* as a classification for federal tax purposes. An *LLC* business entity must file a corporation, partnership, or sole proprietorship tax return.

A few types of businesses generally cannot be *LLCs*, such as banks and insurance companies. Check your state's requirements and the federal tax regulations for further information. Also, there are special rules for foreign *LLCs*.

Low-Profit Limited Liability Company (L3C). An *L3C* is an alternative business that is a hybrid between an *LLC* and non-profit. It is ideal for for-profit entities that have a social mission as their primary vision. According to *Americans for Community Development,* *"the L3C is a brand which signifies to the world that it puts mission before profit yet is self-sustaining."*[80]

Corporations (S & C). There are two types of corporations:

- *C-Corporations* entails prospective shareholders exchanging money, property, or both, for the corporation's capital stock. A corporation generally takes the same deductions as a sole proprietorship to figure its taxable income. A corporation can also take special deductions. For federal income tax purposes, a *C-corporation* is recognized as a separate taxpaying entity. A corporation conducts business, realizes net income or loss, pays taxes, and distributes profits to shareholders. The profit of a corporation is taxed to the corporation when earned, and then it is taxed to the shareholders when distributed as dividends. This creates a double tax. The corporation does not get a tax deduction when it distributes dividends to shareholders. Shareholders cannot deduct any losses of the corporation. They can be publicly or privately held. *C-corporations* are usually larger production, revenue generating businesses like *Wal-Mart, Apple, AT&T,* etc. However, smaller businesses do opt to form *C-corporations*.

- *S-Corporations* are corporations that elect to pass corporate income, losses, deductions, and credit through to their shareholders for federal tax purposes. Shareholders of *S-corporations* report the flow-through of income and losses on their personal tax returns and are assessed tax at their individual income tax rates. This allows *S-corporations* to avoid double taxation on the corporate income. *S-corporations* are responsible for tax on certain built-in gains and passive income. To qualify for *S-corporation* status, the corporation must meet the following requirements:

- Be a domestic corporation.

- Have only allowable shareholders, including individuals, certain trust, and estates and may not include partnerships, corporations, or non-resident alien shareholders.

- Have no more than 100 shareholders.

- Have one class of stock.

- Not be an ineligible corporation (i.e., certain financial institutions, insurance companies, and domestic international sales corporations).

Non-Profit. To be tax-exempt under section 501(c)(3) of the *Internal Revenue Code*, an organization must be organized and operated exclusively for exempt purposes set forth in section 501(c)(3), and none of its earnings may inure to any private shareholder or individual. In addition, it may not be an action organization (*i.e., it may not attempt to influence legislation as a substantial part of its activities, and it may not participate in any campaign activity for or against political candidates*).

Organizations described in section 501(c)(3) are commonly referred to as charitable organizations. Organizations described in section 501(c)(3), other than testing for public safety organizations, are eligible to receive tax-deductible contributions in accordance with *Code Section 170.*

The organization **must not** be organized or operated for the benefit of private interests, and no part of a section 501(c)(3) organization's net earnings may inure to the benefit of any private shareholder or individual. If the organization engages in an excess benefit transaction with a person having substantial influence over the organization, an excise tax may be imposed on the person and any organization managers agreeing to the transaction.

Some examples of 501(c)(3)s are community-based organizations, churches, youth sports programs, charities, and foundations.

It is highly recommended that you seek advice from an attorney that specializes in business structures before finalizing any structure.

EIN. An *Employer Identification Number (EIN)* is a nine-digit number assigned by the IRS. *EINs* are used by employers, some sole proprietors, corporations, partnerships, limited liability companies, estates, trusts, and other entities.

You are required to have an *EIN* if you do one or more of the following:

- Pay wages to one or more employees.

- Operate your business as a corporation or partnership.

- File an employment, excise, pension, alcohol, tobacco, or firearms tax return.

You can apply for your *EIN* online, via phone, mail, or fax. Visit the *IRS* website for more information.

Insurance. Will you need insurance? Insurance protects your organization against claims and risks. There are various types of insurance:

- **Professional Liability Insurance.** Also known as *Errors and Omissions* insurance is the most critical coverage. It protects management and the business from potentially catastrophic litigation caused by charges of professional negligence or failure to perform professional duties. This might include errors and omissions resulting in the loss of client data, software, or system failure, claims of non-performance, or negligent oversell.

- **General (Umbrella) Liability Insurance.** Covers claims of bodily injury or other physical injury or property damage. It is frequently offered in a package with property insurance to protect the business against incidents that may occur on organization premises or at other covered locations where business is normally conducted.

- **Commercial General Liability Insurance.** Enables the business to continue operations while it faces real or fraudulent claims of certain types of negligence or wrongdoing (*i.e., someone gets injured while at an event*).

- **Worker's Comp Insurance.** Once the organization hires employees, state law requires worker's comp insurance to cover those employees. Through the coverage, employers receive assurance that they will not be sued for damages, medical care, and lost wages if employee(s) get injured while working. This type of insurance is not required for members of an *LLC*; however, members can be added to the policy.

I highly recommend that you speak with a reputable insurance agent to help you determine your needs.

Security. When thinking about security, consider having protection for not only theft of office supplies, equipment, inventory, but also theft of your organization's and clients' sensitive information. Identity theft is a major concern in security. Therefore, responsible organizations that collect sensitive information from clients take security seriously. They understand it is crucial to both protect and have a plan in place in the event of a security breach.

If you are just starting out, you may want to limit the amount of sensitive information collected from clients. In addition, having a shredder or using a reputable shredding service is a simple way to dispose of such information if necessary.

Startup Costs. There will be costs associated with launching your vision. Some common startup costs include:

Advertising/Marketing	Brand Development	Consulting Fees/Wages
Equipment & Supplies	Franchise Fees	Incorporation Fees
Insurance	Inventory	Lawyer & Accountant Fees
Licenses and Permits	Office Space	Shipping
Telecommunications	Travel	Utilities
Vehicles/ Transportation	Website Development	Working Capital

✎ DESTINY STARTER™ WORKBOOK

See Activity Seven (7) in the *Destiny Starter™ Workbook* to start writing your plan.

CHAPTER EIGHT:

YOUR BRAND MATTERS

Brand is the promise, the big idea, the expectations that reside in each customer's mind about a product, service or company. Branding is about making an emotional connection.[81]
– Alina Wheeler

A s we've already discussed, your *Call* is linked to a business, ministry, movement, cause, or career. And with each of those, it is highly recommended that you create a brand (*or have one created for you*) – even if the brand is *You*.

So, what is a brand?

BRAND DEFINED[82]

According to Investopedia, a brand is seen as one of its company's most valuable assets. It represents the face of the company, the recognizable logo, slogan, or mark that the public associates with the company. In fact, the company is often referred to by its brand, and they become one and the same.

Here we will use a straightforward brand strategy to help you easily develop your brand. As Alina Wheeler stated in her book, *Designing Brand Identity*, "*an effective brand strategy provides a central, unifying idea around which all behavior, actions and communications are aligned.*"[81]

There are three (3) components of a brand that will be used to create your brand strategy: (1) Messaging, (2) Identity, and (3) Delivery. We will discuss these components separately for both your personal brand and your business brand.

DEVELOPING YOUR PERSONAL BRAND

There is a difference in the brand that you create for yourself and the brand that you create for a business. In this section, we discuss the brand of *You*. We all have a personal brand whether we intentionally create it ourselves or allow others to create it for us. Therefore, independent of whether you have or are planning to start a business, or are working as an employee, developing your personal brand is still important.

Everyone is unique in their own way, maybe you are eccentric or a bit quirky, or maybe you are a bit like me, hard on the outside, but soft on the inside – I suggest that you embrace who you are and be OK sharing a bit of your uniqueness inside your personal brand. We all recognize and respond more favorably to people who are authentic – so I believe it's OK to let the world experience the real you.

So, how do you get started developing your personal brand?

NUMBER ONE: PERSONAL BRAND MESSAGING

Under personal brand messaging, we tune in on the language or voice that you portray to the public. You want to try and make this message as consistent as possible. So, let's get started:

Name

Many people use different names for various reasons. For instance, when my first niece was born, my mom gave her the nickname Muffy. Her government issued name is Alexandra, but from the day she was born, until now, at the age of 25, she still is Muffy. That nickname is constant in all aspects of her life and is ingrained inside her personal brand.

I go by Anita "AC" Clinton – AC was a nickname given to me when I became a loan originator years ago. We had two (2) Anita's in the mortgage office, and initially, when clients would call, if they didn't have our last names, we would do this song and dance trying to figure out which Anita they were calling for. So, to make things a bit easier, collectively we decided I would use my initials, AC. And, today, because some people know me as Anita and others know me by AC, I choose to use both inside my personal brand. In addition, if there's another Anita Clinton out there – because I use "AC" – there will less likely be any confusion between us.

Whatever name you decide to use for your personal brand, be sure to consider all possible factors, such as:

- Is the name appropriate for the persona you want to portray to the public? (*i.e., maybe Pookie isn't appropriate if you are looking to be a partner in a law firm, but Pookie could work if you are Called to the entertainment industry.*)

- Is the name fairly easy to pronounce, and if not, what are some alternatives? (*i.e., I have a client named Nikotris and she recognizes that it's not the easiest name to pronounce correctly. Therefore, her brand includes the pronunciation of her name. It reads, Nikotris (ni • KÄH • tris).*)

- Are there others using the same name? If so, what adjustments can you make to differentiate you from them? Maybe you include your middle name, add a suffix (Jr., Sr., PhD) or catchphrase like Charlamagne tha God, or Cedric the Entertainer. (*i.e., I have a friend named Brandi who is a media producer and musician, and she uses her middle name, Iberia, in her personal brand.*)

Whatever name you choose, the key is that you own it and consistently use it.

Personal Brand Statement

A personal brand statement is a 1-2 sentence statement that summarizes what you do and whom you do it for.

Does this sound familiar?

Back in *Chapter 3*, you created your ZOG *Statement*, and as I mentioned, this statement has many uses. Therefore, there's no need to reinvent the wheel here – your ZOG *Statement* now becomes your personal brand statement.

Personal Mantra, Tagline, or Catchphrase

Consider creating a personal mantra, tagline, or catchphrase for your personal brand. It should be short, catchy, and memorable, and it can be a summarization of your ZOG *Statement*, which describes who you are, and/or what you do. For instance, years ago when I originated mortgages, my catchphrase was the *The Connector*. I connected aspiring homeowners and investors with mortgages that met their needs. I have another friend, Kelly D. Terry, whose tagline is 4 words: *Teach. Inspire. Motivate. Empower.*

Core Values

Your core values articulate the beliefs and principles you live by or what you stand for. It is the scope by which your actions, behaviors, and decisions are viewed through before implementation. It also influences how others perceive your brand.

You want to define 5-7 core values for your personal brand. For me, my personal and business values are the same: honesty, integrity, excellence, fairness, knowledge, innovation, and success. *(See the values template in the Destiny Starter™ Workbook.)*

NUMBER TWO: PERSONAL BRAND IDENTITY

Personal brand identity includes the visual aspects of your brand. It is estimated that non-verbal communication accounts for 60-65 percent of all communication.[83] There are several components that form your brand identity and they include: colors, possibly a logo, and pictures.

Colors

Did you know that colors have meaning? And because they have meaning, they are also memorable and spark emotions. Where your personal brand is concerned, you should consider defining 1 or 2 primary colors that will be used consistently throughout your brand. This doesn't mean they are the only colors you will ever use, but they will be your primary colors. *(See the Meaning of Colors under the Developing Your Business Brand section, page 120.)*

Possible Logo

A logo isn't necessary for a personal brand, but it could definitely be the icing on the cake. There are a couple of things to consider when talking about creating a logo: font, symbol and icon. I break these down in greater detail under the *Developing Your Business Brand* section on page 122.

SAMPLE PERSONAL BRAND LOGO

Source: Anita Clinton Enterprises, LLC.

Pictures and Images

It has been said that an image is worth a thousand words, and you never get a second chance to make a first impression. With that being said, the images that you portray in your personal brand are important. Depending on the arena you find yourself in or are pursuing, it's vital that your image aligns with it. One thing that you definitely want to know is the expected dress code for your field. For instance, if your goal is to be a high-powered corporate attorney, the pictures and images you display should be high-quality and professional.

Thought leader and marketing expert, Seth Godin, is known for his yellow, sometimes purple or blue, framed glasses. If you *Google* his name, and select images, you will see his bald head and the glasses on every photo of him, as well as his colorful tops and ties. His easily recognizable appearance is typically professional, but always with a splash of color.

I recommend once you determine the image for your personal brand, that you have a professional photoshoot annually or bi-annually. You want to have several changes during the photoshoot to ensure you have a variety of pictures that you can use throughout the year. In addition, you want to be considerate of that image as you are taking selfies and appearing in pictures with others. In other words, that image becomes your norm.

NUMBER THREE: PERSONAL BRAND DELIVERY

Personal brand delivery is the last piece of your personal brand that we will discuss here. Although brand delivery methods may vary depending on what you are doing, there are some basic components that I recommend: resume/CV, website, and marketing materials. In addition, to reiterate, the look and feel of your personal brand should be consistent throughout.

Resume or Curriculum Vitae (CV)

This component may not be as important if your *Call* entails you working for yourself. However, if your *Call* entails you working for someone else, maintaining an updated resume or CV is vital. No job is ever secure, therefore you want to stay prepared if needed.

So, what's the difference between a resume and a CV?

Both resumes and CVs are designed to exhibit your work and volunteer experience, skills, education, achievements, interests, and career goals. A resume is a summary of those items, while a CV is a more detailed, comprehensive version of those items. A resume is usually 1-2 pages in length, while a CV has an unlimited length. Both should include the following:

Contact Information. Includes your full name, address, telephone number(s), and email address.

Title. The title should align with the job position you are seeking. You may even adjust the title to fit specific jobs you are applying for.

Summary. The summary should highlight your core competencies and how they would benefit the employer reading your resume. Back in the day we called this the *objective* and it focused on the jobseeker's wants and needs, but today, this *summary* is all about what's in it for the employer. Essentially, it should summarize how your ZOG benefits the employer.

Work and Volunteer Experience. This section will list your work, gigs, internship and/or volunteer experience from the past 10 years. If you don't have experience, you want to place more emphasis on your skills and education. List them in chronological order.

Skills. Here you will list your relevant hard and soft skills. Hard skills are those that you have acquired through education and training. A few examples of hard skills would be computer programming, technical writing, design, etc. Soft skills are your natural abilities. A few examples of soft skills would be attention to detail, leadership, problem solving, etc. In this book, we refer to these collectively as your genius.

Education. This section will portray the education, training, licenses, and certifications that you have obtained. List them in chronological order.

Achievements and Awards. The ultimate goal of your resume or CV is for you to stand out among other candidates. Therefore, you definitely want to include any relevant achievements or awards that you have obtained.

Hobbies and Interests. Do you enjoy camping, playing video games, music, traveling, pets, etc.? In this section, you have an opportunity to share a bit about you personally.

Portfolio. If you are a creative and are applying for a creative position, you should include samples of your work. If you are writing a resume, maybe include a website link to where examples of your work are stored. *(i.e., using GoogleDrive, Dropbox, iCloud, Evernote, etc.)* If you are writing a CV, include visuals of your work inside the CV.

Once you have the components of your resume and CV together, next you want to create a supporting cover letter template. The template will include the basic information that you update in order to customize the content to align with the specific job you are applying for.

You want to open with addressing the letter to the specific person reviewing your resume, if at all possible. This should be followed with an introduction that explains your interest in the position. Next, you want to share why you are the perfect candidate for the job. Here, you want to use bullet points that align with the organization's job requirements. Your qualifications with those requirements should be on full display.

Lastly, close out your letter with a polite call-to-action. The *Jobscan Blog*[84] suggests something like the following:

- "I am keen on meeting with you to see what I can contribute to XYZ company as it moves on in its journey to XYZ goal. I am available at your convenience for a phone call or in-person meeting."

- "I would love to get your thoughts on what I mentioned. I am happy to hop on a phone call at your earliest convenience to discuss how I can help XYZ company with XYZ issue."

Now let's shift the focus to the design. The design of resumes and CVs have come a long way from basic text in a *Microsoft Word* document. It is just another component that could possibly set you apart from other applicants. The design elements should be consistent on both your cover letter and resume or CV. *(See the sample resume on the next page, and in the Destiny Starter™ Workbook for additional resources.)*

Website

A website for your personal brand is optional; however, at the bare minimum, I recommend that you purchase your name's domain *(website address)* whether you have plans to use it or not. You want to own it in the event you need it one day. I have owned www.anitaclinton.com for over 20 years.

If your plan is to blog, vlog, or podcast – it would be greatly beneficial to have a website. There are several options to get you started and I go through them in the *Destiny Starter™ Workbook*. In addition, I share more details about websites under the *Developing Your Business Brand* section on page 126. *(See the sample website after the sample resume on the following pages.)*

Social Media

As I'm sure you know, social media is a huge part of our day-to-day lives. And when we talk about the delivery of your public image, social media will definitely be included in the discussion. Each platform has

SAMPLE RESUME

What's Your VISION?
Let's Manifest It!
Designer • Entrepreneur • Writer

📞 414.206.3399   ✉ anitac@anitaclinton.com   🌐 anitaclinton.com

PROFESSIONAL PROFILE

A hardworking, dedicated designer with a proven record in problem solving, customer satisfaction, graphic/web design, creative writing/editing, and desktop publishing. A leader with the ability to create, organize and enhance presentations, proposals, training programs and marketing material.

- **Desktop Publishing/Design** – 10 years of desktop publishing/design experience with magazines, brochures, flyers, presentations, proposals, newsletters, and other marketing materials.
- **Customer Service** – Solid background with over 20 years of customer service experience. Highly developed communication and negotiation skills.
- **Writing/Editing** – Effective technical writer, copy editor and creative writer. Experience with writing and editing articles, biographies/resumes, manuals, e-books, etc.

SKILLS

Graphic Design	●●●●●●●●●●
Website Design	●●●●●●●●●●
Content Creation & Design	●●●●●●●●●●

SOFTWARES

Illustrator	●●●●●●●●●●
Photoshop	●●●●●●●●●●
InDesign	●●●●●●●●●●
PowerPoint	●●●●●●●●●●
Word	●●●●●●●●●●
Excel	●●●●●●●●●●

PROFESSIONAL EXPERIENCE

WILLIAMS LEA/BAIRD   2008-Present
Desktop Publisher/Presentation Specialist

Responsibilities include PowerPoint presentation creation, extensive graphing and charting in Excel, and general desktop publishing duties for an investment banking firm.

- Produce high-quality pitchbooks, presentations, and memoranda for clients.
- Import and revise graphic files as necessary.
- Create and edit multi-page/multi-section documents using templates and style sheets for pitchbooks, graphs, charts, presentations and other print/design projects.
- Proofread completed projects to ensure quality and accuracy.
- Collaborate with team members on complex or special projects.
- Maintain all job and production tracking data.
- Handle sensitive and/or confidential documents and information.
- Communicate with manager and client on job or deadline issues.

MAGAZINE EXPERIENCE

INVEST WITH PASSION MAGAZINE
Editor/Writer/Graphic Designer

Media entity that produced and published a bi-monthly print magazine, and hosted bi-monthly educational workshops for real estate investors. Co-managed all aspects of editorial and design creation, production, and distribution.

wakeUPgirl MAGAZINE
Editor/Writer/Graphic Designer

Print and digital bi-monthly magazine designed to "sound the alarm for Women to WAKE UP to their greatness." Managed all aspects of editorial and design creation, and production.

EDUCATION & TRAINING

UNIVERSITY OF ILLINOIS
Bachelor of Science

WORLD BIBLE TRAINING INSTITUTE
Certified Minister

CORNELL UNIVERSITY
Certificate of Women's Entrepreneurship

INTERESTS

Reading   Writing   Speaking

Volunteering   Learning   Problem-Solving

REFERENCES

Available upon request.

📍   Milwaukee WI 53202

SAMPLE PERSONAL BRAND WEBSITE

Source: Anita Clinton Enterprises, LLC.

its pros and cons; therefore, you need to determine which will work best for you and your brand.

In addition, each platform generally allows you to fully customize the look of your page or account. This look should fully represent the personal brand you are creating, and you may want to hire a professional graphic designer to design a custom graphic. There are also other do-it-yourself design options available as well. *(See the Destiny Starter™ Workbook for my recommendations.)*

Whether you create or outsource the creation of your graphics, you want to know the size dimensions and specifications for their cover and post graphic. Type **social media dimensions** in the search engine of your choice to see a breakdown of the current dimensions and specifications.

SAMPLE PERSONAL BRAND SOCIAL MEDIA GRAPHIC

Source: Anita Clinton Enterprises, LLC.

* * *

As you advance forward inside fulfilling the *Call* on your life, intentionally managing your public perception is important. This is achieved through creating your personal brand. Inside your personal brand, you want to ensure that you deliver a clean, simple, clear, and consistent message across the board.

DEVELOPING YOUR BUSINESS BRAND

If you have or are planning to start a business *(we will use the term "business" moving forward to represent business, ministry, movement or cause collectively)*, developing your business brand is a necessity. Your business brand must be consistent and works across all your products, services, or programs. It is effective over time and resonates with both your internal and external audience: team, clients, customers, supporters, or followers. Inside your brand strategy, you want to *"see the world through the customer's eyes:"* [81]

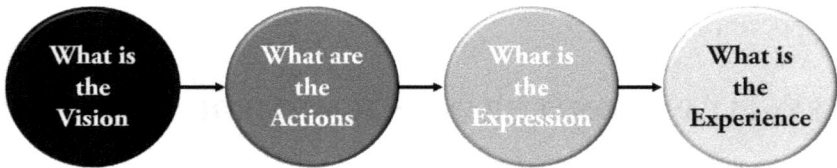

For example, when we look at the *Disney* brand, there's no disputing the fact that they have developed an unforgettable, laser-focused brand. If you were to do a search on *YouTube* for *Disney World* commercials, you will get a wide array of options. However, the underlying brand is the same, and it's very consistent throughout all marketing and promotions. We will examine the *Disney* brand in further detail as we go through the three (3) components of building your business brand strategy: (1) Messaging, (2) Identity, and (3) Delivery.

NUMBER ONE: BUSINESS BRAND MESSAGING

Under brand messaging, we tune in on the language or voice that you use to connect with your audience. It is crucial that the message is consistent across the board...essentially, it will be used in some form or fashion in all communications. So, let's get started:

Organization Name

The name of your business is the first part of your brand messaging. Your name should be timeless, simple, and memorable. It can be a namesake, abbreviation, acronym, oxymoron, descriptive, etc. Your name should have meaning for you and it should be something that your audience will easily understand and resonate with. In addition, the more you can describe what you do inside the name, the better.

For instance, the *Disney* name is based on its founder's name, *Walt Disney*, and it has become synonymous with paradise, magic, fun, and winning. On the flip side, if we look at the company name Netflix, it brilliantly describes what it is - flicks or flixs as the company spells it *(movies)* on the net *(online)*. Another example would be Amazon, named after the largest tropical rainforest in the world. In addition, take note of the arrow under *Amazon's* logo, it points from the "A" to the "Z". They are serious about being the largest organization in the world, carrying everything you need from A to Z.

Core Values

As discussed in the previous section, your core values articulate the beliefs and principles you live by or what you stand for. They are the scope by which your actions, behaviors, and decisions are viewed through before implementation. They also influence how others perceive your brand.

You want to define 5-7 core values for your business brand. Like me, your core personal and business values could be the same. Or they can be similar or completely different. You must determine what your business stands for and infuse that throughout every aspect of the business.

Keywords

You want to define 10–20 keywords that describe your business. Look at it this way, if someone was searching for you on *Google*, what keywords would they use? *(For instance, Disney's keywords would possibly be: magical, paradise, family fun, family vacation, theme parks, Mickey Mouse, resorts, animated movies, cartoon characters, kids' games, kids' books, kids' toys, etc.)*

There are several online tools that you can use to expand your search for keywords...simply type **keyword research tool** in the search engine of your choice.

Vision Statement

A vision statement, as defined by Roger Constandse, *"is a vivid idealized description of a desired outcome that inspires, energizes and helps you create a mental picture of your target."*[85] It is based on a combination of your overall vision and your *Why*. It answers the questions:

- Why are you interested in doing this?

- Why does this matter or why is this important?

If you recognize, these are questions you answered back in *Chapter* 6. You will take what you created there to compose your vision statement. It is the composite, the overall big picture, when it's all said and done, what you hope to accomplish in one bold statement. In other words, it states your *Big Audacious Goal* in an amazingly simple and clear manner.

A great example is *Disney's* vision statement, *To Make People Happy!*[86] Every time I see *Disney's* vision statement, I smile. Everything they do is specifically designed with their vision in mind, to make people happy.

Your vision statement will complete the sentence: **In the end, I want to...**

Mission Statement

A mission statement tells how you plan to achieve the vision statement. The mission will portray what the business does and the values *(principles and beliefs)* of the organization. It will drive everything that the organization does moving forward. It is based on the *What* and *How* you created in *Chapter* 6 by answering the following questions:

- What can your target audience expect from you?

- What can your target audience come to you for?

- What challenge(s) or pain(s) are you solving?

- How do you deliver the results?

- How do you answer the challenge(s) or solve the pain(s)?

You will take what you've already created to compose your mission statement. This one may require a little more time and thought; however, I still caution you not to overthink it.

Another great example would be *Disney's* mission statement: *The Mission of the Walt Disney Company is to entertain, inform and inspire people around the globe through the power of unparalleled storytelling, reflecting the iconic brands, creative minds and innovative technologies that make ours the world's premier entertainment company.*[86]

You want to try and keep your mission statement to 1–2 sentences, and it will complete the sentence: **I will achieve the vision by or through...**

EXAMPLE VISION & MISSION STATEMENTS[87]

Business/Ministry: Be Great Global

Vision: We envision a world where 1 billion morally conscious, ethical *Dreamers* are walking boldly in their *Greatness* and transforming the face of our world.

Mission: To serve, support and hold *Dreamers* accountable to discovering, strategizing, and executing the plan for their lives. Through events, materials, and training and development programs, we help *Dreamers* build the infrastructure to live an extraordinary life on *Purpose*.

Movement: Susan G. Komen

Vision: A world without breast cancer.

Mission: At Susan G. Komen, our mission is to save lives by meeting the most critical needs in our communities and investing in breakthrough research to prevent and cure breast cancer.

Cause: Cradles to Crayons

Vision: Cradles to Crayons was shaped by a vision that existing community resources could be leveraged to benefit economically disadvantaged children, bridging the gap between those who have too much and those who do not have enough.

Mission: Cradles to Crayons provides children from birth through age 12, living homeless or low-income situations, with the essential items they need to thrive – at home, at school and at play. We supply these items free of charge by engaging and connecting communities that have with communities that need.

Tagline

Alina Wheeler states, *"A tagline is a short phrase that captures a company's brand essence, personality, and positioning, and distinguishes the company/product from its competitors."*[81] According to Wheeler, taglines can be imperative *(action-related)*, descriptive, superlative *(best-in-class)*, provocative *(questionable)*, or specific to a category. You want to keep it short and simple, and it should evoke an emotional response.

For example, *Disneyland's* tagline is *The Happiest Place on Earth*.[88] It's short, sweet, to the point, and once again, makes me smile.

For your tagline, try to describe your *What* in the shortest sentence or words possible. Essentially, you can take your mission statement and trim it down to a simple, short, clear and concise message that will evoke an emotion.

EXAMPLE TAGLINES[89]

Imperative *(Actionable)*

Apple: Think Different

GoPro: Be a Hero

Nike: Just Do It

YouTube: Broadcast Yourself

Be Great Global: Answer the Call and Love the Work You Do

Lays: Betcha Can't Eat Just One

Descriptive

Allstate: You're in Good Hands

Target: Expect More. Pay Less.

GE: Imagination at Work

Toms: One For One

Superlative *(Best-in-Class)*

BMW: The Ultimate Driving Machine

Canada Goose: Our Uncompromised Craftsmanship Defines Canadian Luxury

DeBeers: A Diamond is Forever

Provocative *(Questionable)*

National Day Council: Got Milk?

Sears: Where Else?

Verizon: Can You Hear Me Now?

Specific *(Category)*

Bounty: The Quicker Picker Upper

Olay: Your Best Beautiful

The New York Times: All The News That's Fit To Print

Volkswagen: Drivers Wanted

Value Proposition

Your value proposition will provide a clear statement of the tangible results your target audience obtains from your business. It tells what problem or pain point your ventures solves, and defines the value added.

For instance, *Disney's* value proposition *is wherever the Guest experience takes place – in our parks, on the high seas, on a guided tour of exotic locales, through our vacation ownership program – we remain dedicated to the promise that our Cast members turn the ordinary into the extraordinary. Making dreams come true every day is central to our global growth strategy.*[90]

Because I know value propositions are not the easiest to create, let's dissect *Disney's*. It begins referencing their target audience, whom they call "guests." In alignment with their vision *to make people happy* – everything they do is about their guests' experience wherever it happens on their watch. Next, they highlight their promise, that everyone on their team follows, whom they refer to as *Cast members*, – *to turn the ordinary into the extraordinary*. And then ends with a further declaration to the guest experience of *making dreams come true every day*. It is noticeably clear here that *Disney's* value proposition is all about their target audience having an amazing experience when they buy their products or services.

EXAMPLE VALUE PROPOSITIONS[91]

Be Great Global
We take the worry out of you not knowing the *Call* on your life, the anxiety out of how to do what you've been *Called* to do, and the fear of doing it all alone. So come on, let's do this!

Stripe
The New Standard in Online Payments. Stripe is the best software platform for running an internet business. We handle billions of dollars every year for forward-thinking businesses around the world.

Evernote
Meet Evernote, your anywhere access notepad. Capture, organize, and share notes from anywhere. Your best ideas are always with you and always in sync.

Fundly
Raise Money for Anything. Fundly is fast, easy and has no raise requirements.

Hubspot
Grow Your Business. More than 11,500 companies in 70 countries use HubSpot's marketing and sales software to grow.

Unique Selling Proposition (USP)

As defined by entrepreneur.com, a unique selling proposition is *"the factor or consideration presented by a seller as the reason that one product or service is different from and better than that of the competition."*[92] Essentially, it is a 1-2 sentence statement around what makes your business different from others. It answers the question, *What is the unique thing/element that your target   audience can only get from you?*

According to Alina Wheeler[81], your *USP* will typically fall into 1 of 3 areas: Quality, Price, and/or Service.

EXAMPLE UNIQUE SELLING PROPOSITIONS[81]

QUALITY: M&M's
The milk chocolate melts in your mouth, not in your hand.

PRICE: Geico
Switching to *Geico* could save you 15% or more on your car insurance.

SERVICE: FedEx
When it absolutely, positively has to be there overnight.

Be Great Global's USP is *"We help Dreamers use their Superpower to live an extraordinary life and transform the face of the world, using the Destiny Starter™ System."* My target audience can't get the *Destiny Starter™ System* from no other company but mine. It is the unique element that we bring to the marketplace.

Elevator Pitch

The last part of your messaging that we will discuss is your elevator pitch. Your elevator pitch should be 1–2 sentences that tell who your target audience is and what you do for them to make their lives better. You should memorize your elevator pitch so that it flows off your tongue with ease when needed.

There are various types of elevator pitches...however, I recommend that you use the one that you have already created called your ZOG *Statement* and your *What*.

For example, *Be Great Global's* elevator pitch is: *I help intrapreneurs and entrepreneurs find happiness, fulfillment, and money doing work they actually love.*

On occasion, I use the following: *I help Dreamers discover, strategize, and execute the Call on their lives so they can use their Superpower to live an extraordinary life and transform our world.*

NUMBER TWO: BUSINESS BRAND IDENTITY

Brand identity is an important component of an organization's overall brand. It is the visual representation of an organization's DNA. Therefore, a well-designed brand identity supports and portrays the culture, value, and purpose of the organization. It helps to distinguish you from everyone else.

There are several components that form your brand identity and they include: color scheme, logo, and stationery. Essentially, your brand speaks before you open your mouth, and you want to ensure that it is memorable.

<u>Color Scheme</u>

As stated previously, colors have meaning. The colors you choose for your business are important and they also psychologically speak for it. You want to create a color scheme consisting of 4–6 colors that will be used consistently throughout your brand. Take the time to define your colors and be sure not to deviate from them inside your overall brand. This doesn't mean they are the only colors you will ever use, but they will be your primary colors.

On the next couple of pages, you will find the meaning of some basic colors to help you narrow down your brand's color scheme.

MEANING OF COLORS

Red
Energy, Passion, Action, Strength, Excitement, Attention-Getting, Intense, Fire, Blood, Danger

Orange
Cheerful, Happy, Optimistic, Logical, Confidence, Analytical, Warm, Stimulating, Creative, Success

Yellow
Growth, Renewal, Reliability, Tactful, Practical, Compassionate, Sunshine, Joy, Cheerfulness, Intellect, Attention

Green
Communication, Clarity, Balance, Harmony, Creativity, Calmness, Nature, Growth, Healing, Safety, Money, Fresh

Blue
Loyalty, Integrity, Responsibility, Orderly, Peace, Devotion, Sky, Sea, Depth, Stability, Trust, Tranquil

Pink
Unconditional, Compassion, Nurturing, Warmth, Hope, Love, Truth, Affection, Ethereal, Peace

Purple
Unusual, Individual, Intuitive, Humanitarian, Royalty, Mystery, Power, Wealth, Ambition, Dignified

Brown
Earth, Inexpensive, Simplicity, Comfort, Longevity, Masculine, Nurturing, Contentment, Productivity

Black
Authority, Power, Control, Serious, Sophisticated, Dignified, Formal

White
Innocence, Purity, Cleanliness, Simplicity, Equality, Neat, Peace, Reverence, Holiness, Innovation

Grey
Security, Reliability, Intelligence, Modesty, Quiet, Quality, Conservativeness, Practical

MEANING OF COLORS

Gold
Success, Achievement, Triumph, Abundance, Prosperity, Luxury, Quality, Prestige, Elegance

Silver
Feminine Energy, Fluid, Emotional, Sensitive, Mysterious, Calm, Soothing, Purifying, Hi-Tech, Sleek

Bronze
Unconditional, Compassion, Nurturing, Warmth, Hope, Love

Copper
Strength, Malleability, Ductility, Passion, Professional Growth, Business Productivity

I recommend that you start with no more than 1 or 2 primary colors. Then, type **[your primary color] color schemes** in *Google's* search engine *(i.e., pink and green color schemes)*. Next you want to click **images** and you will get a visual of various color schemes to help you finalize the remaining colors. For your convenience, I also included links to a color wheel and possible schemes in the *Destiny Starter™ Workbook*. The final scheme should consist of 4–6 colors.

SEARCH ENGINE SNAPSHOT

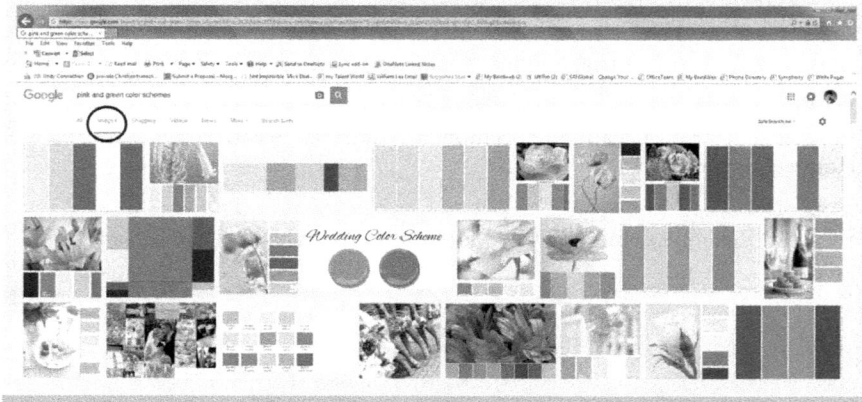

For the 4-6 colors that you designate, you want to pinpoint and record your colors RGB, HEX, and CMYK codes. You will use these codes when you are having any type of graphics designed.

- **RGB** = Red, Green, Blue and range between 0–255 (*0=black and 255=white*).

- **HEX** = a hex triplet is a six-digit, three-byte hexadecimal number used in HTML, CSS, SVG, and other computing applications to represent colors (*mostly used on the internet*). The bytes represent the red, green, and blue components of the colors and they range from 00–FF, and there's usually a hashtag (#) before the characters[93] (*i.e., #000000=black and #ffffff=white*).

- **CMYK** = The CMYK color model (*process color, four color*) is a subtractive color model, typically used in professional color printing, and is also used to describe the printing process itself. CMYK refers to the four inks used during color printing: cyan, magenta, yellow, and key (*or black*).

To pinpoint your color codes, type **RGB, HEX, CMYK Conversion Tool** into the search engine of your choice and select the tool that will allow you to obtain the codes for your colors. If you are working with professional designers, they will usually provide this information for you in what's called a *brand identity guide (see the example on page 124).* If not, be sure to ask them to provide one. It comes in handy when working with other designers to ensure your brand remains consistent.

Logo

Your business logo is the graphical mark or symbol that you use to visually portray your brand. It will utilize your color scheme and should be professionally designed, if possible. There are a couple of things to consider where your logo is concerned – the font, symbol, and icon:

Font. There are four basic types of fonts: (1) serif, (2) sans serif, (3) script, and (4) decorative. A **serif** is a short line at the edges of the font. The font you are looking at now is a serif font called Goudy Old Style; others include **Times Roman** or Garamond.

Sans serif is a font without serifs – sans means *"without"*. Examples of sans serif fonts include Arial, Century Gothic, **Tahoma**, and Calibri.

Script fonts include strokes that are typically derived by cursive handwriting. Examples of script fonts are *Brush Script*, *Edwardian Script*, and *Monotype Corsiva.*

Lastly, *decorative* fonts are fancy, more creative fonts that are typically used for titles and headlines. Examples of decorative fonts are Buckwheat TC, *Magneto* and True Sketch.

Symbol or Icon. Some logos only utilize text or font; however, other logos use or include a symbol or icon. Take the *Apple* logo for example, it is simply an apple with a bite out of it. You can choose to incorporate a symbol or icon that has special meaning for or complements your brand.

EXAMPLE LOGOS

San Serif & Decorative Fonts with a Symbol

Script & San Serif

San Serif & Decorative Fonts with a Symbol

Source: Anita Clinton Enterprises, LLC.

EXAMPLE BRAND IDENTITY GUIDE

BRAND IDENTITY GUIDE

BE GRE**X**T
Global

1. GRAPHICAL MARK

ICON	FULL LOGO	ALTERNATIVE LOGO

BE GRE**X**T
Global

2. VARIATIONS

The Be Great Global (BGG) was designed with multiple variations:

Icon Only Logo
The icon only version of the logo will be used as deemed necessary. Be sure to maintain the proportions of the logo at all times. Avoid stretching or distorting the logo.

Full Logo
The full version of the logo is ideal for instances when there are no space limitations. Be sure to maintain the proportions of the logo at all times. Avoid stretching or distorting the logo.

Alternative Logo
The alternative version of the logo will most likely be used when space is limited. Be sure to maintain the proportions of the logo at all times. Avoid stretching or distorting the logo.

3. COLORS

The BGG brand is made up of six colors that should be dominant across all branded collateral:

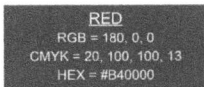

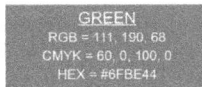

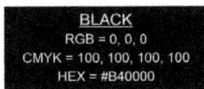

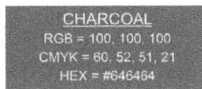

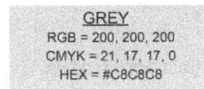

RED	GREEN	BLUE
RGB = 180, 0, 0	RGB = 111, 190, 68	RGB = 0, 0, 255
CMYK = 20, 100, 100, 13	CMYK = 60, 0, 100, 0	CMYK = 88, 77, 0, 0
HEX = #B40000	HEX = #6FBE44	HEX = #0000FF

BLACK	CHARCOAL	GREY
RGB = 0, 0, 0	RGB = 100, 100, 100	RGB = 200, 200, 200
CMYK = 100, 100, 100, 100	CMYK = 60, 52, 51, 21	CMYK = 21, 17, 17, 0
HEX = #B40000	HEX = #646464	HEX = #C8C8C8

4. TYPOGRAPHY

ARIAL	GABRIOLA
ABCDEFGHIJKLMNOPQRSTUVWXYZ	ABCDEFGHIJKLMNOPQRSTUVWXYZ
abcdefghijklmnopqrstuvwxyz	abcdefghijklmnopqrstuvwxyz

www.begreatglobal.com

Source: Anita Clinton Enterprises, LLC.

There are several cost-effective platforms *(as low as $5.00)* that you can utilize to have your logo designed. In addition, there are some free tools, all of which are accessible by typing **logo design** into the search engine of your choice. I also list viable options in the *Destiny Starter™ Workbook.*

When having your logo professionally designed, in addition to the standard .jpeg and .png files, you also want to request a vector file. This file format will be .eps, .ai, .svg or .psd. You may not be able to open this file, but it will be used anytime you are having something professionally designed or printed. In addition, you also want to ask for the font files or, at the bare minimum, the name of the fonts used to create the logo. For designers, these files are especially important. *(See the example on brand identity guide on the previous page.)*

Stationery

All your business correspondence should be presented professionally using branded stationery. Your stationery includes letterheads, envelopes, and business cards.

Whether you are communicating via email or snail mail – you want to present a professional presentation, because it's important!

As with your logo, you can have your stationery professionally designed or you can find free templates online by typing **brand stationery templates** in the search engine of your choice.

Upon receiving the final designs from a professional designer, be sure to request a digital version of your letterhead setup in *Microsoft Word* or whatever word processing program you use. This file will come in handy when you are sending digital letters or documents, because it keeps you on brand.

EXAMPLE STATIONERY

Business Card Design   Letterhead Design

Source: Anita Clinton Enterprises, LLC.

NUMBER THREE: BUSINESS BRAND DELIVERY

The last piece of your brand that we will discuss here is brand delivery. Although brand delivery methods may vary depending on what you are doing, there are some basic components that are standard across the board. They include website, signage, and marketing materials. In addition, if you have a physical product that you are bringing to the marketplace, you will need labeling and packaging designs.

Whether your target audience gets a business card, picks up a brochure, or visits your website, the look and feel of your brand should be consistent throughout.

Website

Every business should have a website. It is your virtual location, accessible to anyone with an internet connection. As of 2020, there were over 7 billion people in the world, and over 50% *(4+ billion)* of them use the Internet.

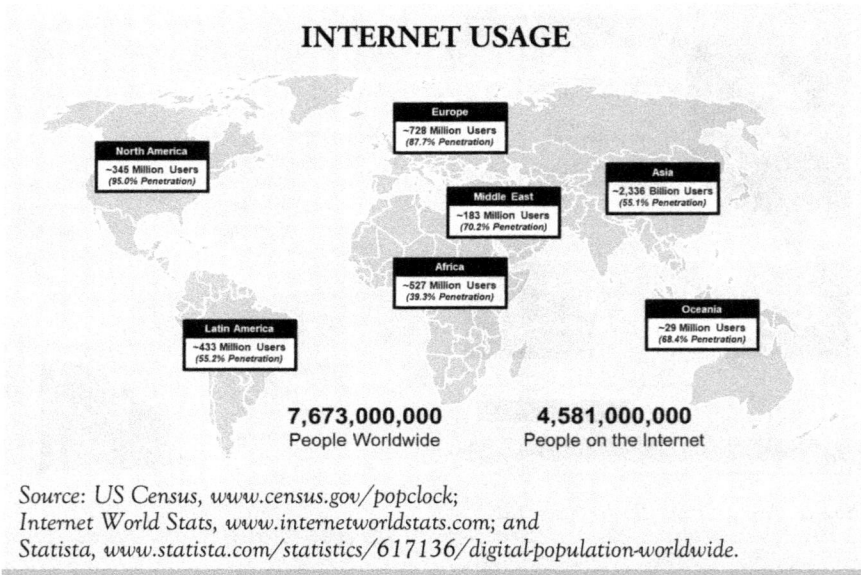

INTERNET USAGE

Europe
~728 Million Users
(87.7% Penetration)

North America
~345 Million Users
(95.0% Penetration)

Asia
~2,336 Billion Users
(55.1% Penetration)

Middle East
~183 Million Users
(70.2% Penetration)

Africa
~527 Million Users
(39.3% Penetration)

Oceania
~29 Million Users
(68.4% Penetration)

Latin America
~433 Million Users
(55.2% Penetration)

7,673,000,000
People Worldwide

4,581,000,000
People on the Internet

Source: US Census, www.census.gov/popclock;
Internet World Stats, www.internetworldstats.com; and
Statista, www.statista.com/statistics/617136/digital-population-worldwide.

You will need to acquire a domain *(website address)* and webhost company for your website. Think of the domain as the address to your house and the webhost company as the land that your house sits on. The domain will run anywhere between $1.99–$25.99 a year. It is especially important that you do not allow your annual domain payment to lapse, because you will lose it. Retrieving your domain can be exceedingly difficult and will typically cost considerably more. In addition to the domain costs, you will also have to pay monthly or annual webhosting fees. They will range between $50–$150 a year.

According to Dan Miller of *Storybrand*,[94] your website should tell visitors:

1. What you offer or sell if you are for profit, or who you are trying to help if you are a non-profit?

2. How it's going to make their life better *(for profit)* or how it's going the make the world better *(non-profit)*?

3. How can they purchase it *(for profit)* or what do I need to do to participate *(non-profit)*?

Your website should be *responsive*, meaning it is mobile-friendly and will adjust to fit all size mobile devices. It should give visitors a clear view and understanding of what you do for them and who you are. They should know your *USP* and *Value Proposition* before leaving the site. In addition, there should be a clear call-to-action: join our mailing list, call us today, get a free estimate, donate, etc. *(See the sample website on the next page.)*

I recommend that your website include the following sections or pages:

About	Contact
Home	Products/Services/Programs

Additional pages could include:

Blog/Vlog/Podcast	Events
FAQ	Gallery
Media	Start Here
Store	Testimonials

A *blog, vlog, or podcast* could be an impactful addition to your website. It affords you an opportunity to connect with your audience on a more intimate and consistent level.

Mobile App

Research shows that 89% of consumers' mobile time is spent on apps.[95] Therefore, it may be highly beneficial to invest in creating a

SAMPLE WEBSITE

Source: Anita Clinton Enterprises, LLC.

mobile app for your business. Mobile app developers, *BuildFire*, highlights the following 3 ways you can benefit from having an app:[96]

- Provide more value to your target audience.
- Build a stronger brand and boost profits.
- Connect better with audience.

Signage

If your business will have a brick-and-mortar location, you will need to obtain external and internal signage. The signage should creatively and attractively represent your brand. In addition, tabletop easels and retractable banners work well for vending tables or other opportunities for you to showcase your products, services, or programs.

EXAMPLE SIGNAGE

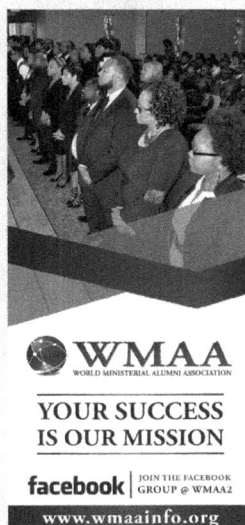

Source: Anita Clinton Enterprises, LLC.

Marketing Materials

Marketing materials include any materials that you will use to advertise and promote your business. There are a couple of marketing materials that I highly recommend you obtain:

One-Sheet. A beautifully designed one- or two-page promotional document that summarizes your *Who, What,* and *How.* Independent of the organization model you choose, I highly recommend you have a one-sheet created. Your one-sheet should include your biography or brief description of your business, products or services, topics or programs, benefits, client list, testimonials or endorsements, and contact information.

Source: Anita Clinton Enterprises, LLC.

Media Kit or Press Kit. The media kit is a more detailed, in-depth version of the one-sheet. Investopedia defines it as *"a promotional public relations tool that can serve several functions, including promoting the* *launch of a new company, promoting the launch of a new product or service by an existing company, giving a company a way to present itself as it would like to be seen, and saving time by eliminating the need for a company's employees to repeatedly answer the same questions."*[97] Your media kit or press kit could include your biography or description of your business, products, services or programs, vision and mission statements, benefits, list of suggested questions for potential interviews, client list, accomplishments, testimonials or endorsements, recent press releases or media mentions, samples of work, photos, links to audio or video, etc.

Investor Kit. Depending on your organization model, raising funds may be necessary to bring your product to the market. Finding potential investors is a viable option and creating a professional investor kit is key. Your investor kit may include a cover letter, a description or profile of you and the business, annual and quarterly financial report summaries, press releases or other media mentions, testimonials or endorsements, interviews, and the investor pitch.

Label and Packaging Graphics. If you have a physical product, you will most likely need labeling and packaging designs. There are several things to consider, including color, imagery, font, design, printed content, size, shape, finishing and material. If you are looking to have your product in stores, be sure that you consider the amount of shelf space required to display your product. It should be large enough to attract attention, but not too large that it takes up considerable space. If you are not looking to have your product in stores but are looking to dropship directly to your customer, you also want to consider how you will ship the product, and the shipping cost per item.

Advertisement Graphics. Advertisement graphics include a wide array of graphics that you will use daily to advertise and promote your business. These include postcards, flyers, posters, social media graphics, infographics, memes, etc.

SAMPLE GRAPHICS

Source: Anita Clinton Enterprises, LLC.

Social Media Graphics. Social media platforms provide great opportunities to promote your business. However, I will caution you that promotion on social media must be combined with both engagement and delivering valuable content.

Each platform generally allows you to fully customize the look of your page or account. In addition, each of them has different size dimensions and specifications. Type **social media dimensions** in the search engine of your choice to see a breakdown of the current dimensions and specifications.

SAMPLE SOCIAL MEDIA GRAPHICS

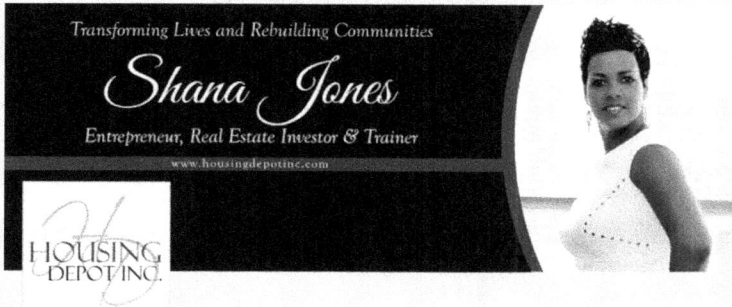

Source: Anita Clinton Enterprises, LLC.

Custom PowerPoint. I believe all businesses should have a custom PowerPoint handy. It can be used for different types of presentations, pitches, proposals, etc.

SAMPLE CUSTOM POWERPOINT

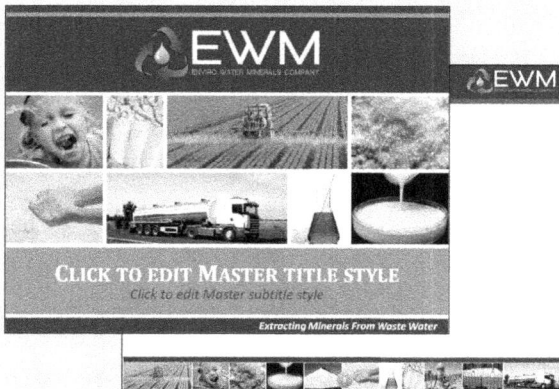

Source: Anita Clinton Enterprises, LLC.

PDFs. From a professional standpoint, be sure to always save your digital files *(letters, PowerPoints, one-sheets, media kits, etc.)* as .pdfs before sending them out. You don't want to send editable documents to customers, clients, potential sponsors, investors, partners, etc. and saving as a .pdf considerably limits editing capabilities. In addition, pdfs are typically easier to open and read on computers, tablets, and other mobile devices.

Other Things to Consider

Depending on your organization model, you may need to utilize one or more of the following:

Exhibits	Forms
Promotional Items	Step & Repeat Banners
Uniforms	Vehicle Identification

● ● ●

In conclusion, your brand is a crucial component to the success of your venture. I can't state it enough: you want to ensure that you deliver a clean, simple, clear and consistent message across the board. You want your audience to not only become familiar with the look and feel of your brand, but you want to evoke an emotional experience as well.

✎ DESTINY STARTER™ WORKBOOK

See Activity Eight (8) in the *Destiny Starter™ Workbook* to develop both personal and business brands. In addition, you will find details and my resources recommendations.

CHAPTER NINE:

SIMPLIFY YOUR MARKETING

The aim of marketing is to know and understand the customer [audience] so well the product or service fits him [her] and sells itself.[98] – Peter Drucker

OK, we are moving right along. Once you've developed your brand, next is creating a marketing plan that will help you spread your message to the world. I want to stress how important it is that you focus on your *What* inside your marketing. What challenge(s) or pain(s) are you solving in the world? That's the focus – your product, service, or program is defined in your *How* and is a byproduct of your *What*. The success of your marketing efforts depends on the clarity in which you can explain how your *What* is the answer to your audience's problem(s).

I understand that effective marketing can be complicated and costly. Whether you are implementing marketing yourself or outsourcing it, my intention is to help simplify the process in a cost-effective manner. There is an old saying that goes cheap, good or fast, you pick two. You can have it done quickly, you can have it done at minimum cost, or you can have it done in excellence, but you can't have all three together.

If we were to apply this concept to your marketing plan, you are either going to:

- Pay a lot of money and get high quality results, while sacrificing speed.

- Pay a lot of money and get it fast, while sacrificing quality.

- Pay little money and hopefully get high quality results, but sacrifice speed.

- Pay little money and get it fast, but sacrifice quality.

Depending on your budget, you have a decision to make based on the concepts above. Independent of the route you choose to take, I have devised this plan to efficiently work either way. If you have more available funds, you can apply less effort and get results. If you have limited funds, with more effort you can still get results. Either way, it all starts with a marketing plan...

COMPOSING YOUR CAREER MARKETING PLAN

For those who are looking to fulfill the *Call* working as an employee, this section is for you. In *Chapter 7* you defined the core elements of your career action plan. Inside of your plan, are your short- and long-term S.M.A.R.T. goals. You will use these goals, along with your knowledge of the specific problem or pain your *Zone of Greatness* (ZOG) solves, to help compose your career marketing plan. This will encompass the following: market analysis and research, marketing strategy, and marketing implementation.

MARKET ANALYSIS & RESEARCH

Depending on the industry you are interested in, an analysis of the market involves:

- Researching potential companies that may be of interest to you, and start building a list of those you would want to work for.

- Researching open job opportunities that align with your ZOG, both where you are currently working and externally.

- Researching the salary range for your perfect position.

- Understanding the trends and economic conditions in your industry. For instance, if your ZOG leads you to the print media industry, you really want to study and understand where you think this industry is going. Maybe you have innovative ideas to revitalize the print media industry and help combat the current enormous shift from print to digital media.

MARKETING STRATEGY

Your marketing strategy will provide details for your marketing efforts. It will include defining your network and promotional options.

<u>Define Your Network</u>

Networking is an important component of your marketing strategy. As defined by *TopResume*, *"Networking is about establishing and nurturing long-term, mutually beneficial relationships with the people you meet, whether you're waiting to order your morning coffee, participating in an intramural sports league, or attending a work conference."*[99] Coauthor of the *Go-Givers* book series, Bob Burg said, *"Networking is simply the cultivating of mutually beneficial, give and take, win-win relationships. It works best, however, when emphasizing the 'give' part."*[100]

For you extraverts out there, networking may be music to your ears. On the flipside, for those introverts like me, networking may not be on the top of your to-do list. Either way, I have created a system to make this process easier for all of us, and it involves dividing your network into three (3) tiers:

Tier 1: Allies. Your allies are those individuals whom you have a personal relationship with, and that relationship has been formed by emotional bonds and interactions. Your allies will consist of your family, friends, mentors, and could even be co-workers that you've built a relationship or friendship with outside of work.

Tier 2: Associates. Your associates are those individuals that you know, and that know you back. So, there's a two-way connection. And although you may not be best friends, you all have had some level of interaction presently or in the past. They are co-workers, managers, people in your social groups or clubs (*i.e., church or Rotary Club, sororities & fraternities, etc.*). In addition, associates can be found in professional or trade organizations, your social media contacts, your or your kids' teachers, professors, college alumni, etc.

Tier 3: Audience. Your audience are those individuals whom you may or may not have met, but you don't know them, and/or they don't know you. These individuals are out there in the audience or in the world, and they have the ability to help you advance your career, but they haven't had the pleasure of meeting or personally connecting with you. Or they are those in the audience or world who have the knowledge and experience that you can access without ever meeting or connecting with them. To complete this tier, it will require you to set aside some time to do some research and identify those individuals who are:

- In the field, doing what you want to do, and doing it exceptionally well.

- In leadership positions at your current job or other organizations.

- Influencers, entrepreneurs, thought leaders.

- You can encounter them while volunteering, networking, on social media platforms like *LinkedIn*, in training or continuing education classes, etc.

- Or you can watch their TV or *YouTube* shows, listen to their podcasts, read their books, take their courses, hire them as coaches, etc.

With this tier, you can, but you don't necessarily have to have a one-on-one relationship or connection with them. You can access their knowledge and experience inside contact with them, or from a distance. For example, Oprah Winfrey and Tony Robbins are in my *Tier 3: Network*, and I can tell you that I have learned more from them than anyone I'm connected to, and I have some pretty strong allies and associates in my network. The same can be true for you.

With that, you want to be sure to take the time to really identify who's who in your network, and then in the next chapter, we discuss what to do with that network.

Define Your Promotional Options

At this point, your cover letter, resume or CV should be complete, so here's how you let potential future employers know you exist:

Referrals. We talked about defining your network above; everyone on your tier 1 and tier 2 list should be notified that you are looking to advance your career. You never know who may know who.

Job Boards and Career Websites. There are a plethora of websites that post job listings. In the *Destiny Starter™ Workbook* you will find my recommendations. I will caution you to consider creating a separate *Gmail* or *Yahoo* email address for these platforms, just in case your email address gets picked up by spammers.

Job Fairs. Job fairs give you an opportunity to meet with multiple employers in one setting. You want to do your research to determine which employers are of interest to you, independent of whether they have an opening for your perfect position or not. If the company is a good fit, you never know what positions may become available in the future or what opportunities may exist to customize a position specifically for you. At the end of the day, you want to arrive early, make the necessary connections, and be sure to follow up afterwards.

Headhunters and Recruiters. Depending on the field you are looking to go into, headhunting and recruiting agencies may be a better option. Headhunters typically work with multiple organizations seeking to fill multiple higher level positions at the same time. While recruiters typically work for one specific organization, and are looking to fill one (1) or more positions within the same organization. It's also very important you know that both are paid by the company upon placement and not by you. Lastly, both are fairly easy to find via platforms like *LinkedIn* and the search engine of your choice.

Social Media. Social media can be a great resource during your job search. If you are in search of a new job, then you should definitely be on *LinkedIn*. I walk you through setting up and updating your *LinkedIn* profile in the *Destiny Starter™ Workbook*. In addition, you want to ensure to update and clean up your profiles and posts (*if applicable*), so that they align with what you are creating and where you want to go. Please know, many of your potential employers will view your social media pages.

MARKETING IMPLEMENTATION

Once you've thought through and recorded your marketing strategy, next is giving thought to how you will execute that strategy like: reaching out to your network, distributing your resume/CV, applying for positions, scheduling interviews, etc. This also includes defining your monthly, weekly, and daily activities, and possible content generation.

Monthly, Weekly, and Daily Activities

Here you want to give thought to your daily, weekly, or monthly activities. Are there specific days that you do certain things? For instance, how many times will you reach out to hiring managers, recruiters, etc., per week? If you take the time to plan this out, it will make things a lot easier and more manageable.

Possible Content Generation

Depending on your area of focus, content marketing may be an added benefit for you. It includes posting on your website, other blogs/websites, social media, podcasting, etc. Generating useful, relevant, entertaining, and inspirational content can appeal to and attract your target audience. If you defined two (2) audiences in the *Who* section, this content would speak to both. I talk more about content generation on page 159.

❋ ❋ ❋

Composing your marketing plan for advancing your career should be relatively easy. The ultimate goal is that you seek and make as many connections as possible. There's a saying I was told years ago, *closed mouths don't get fed*. In other words, you want to open your mouth and share your vision with everyone you encounter.

COMPOSING YOUR BUSINESS MARKETING PLAN

If your *Call* entails running a business *(remember we are using the term "business" to represent business, ministry, movement, or cause collectively)*, this section is for you.

GOALS AND OBJECTIVES

The first component of your business marketing plan entails defining your marketing goals and objectives. This answers the question, what are the results you want to see from your marketing efforts? As stated previously, these goals should be S.M.A.R.T.:

Specific. Clearly define the goal, including actual numbers *(if applicable)* for what you want to accomplish.

Measurable. You want to be able to track the goal, to ensure that it is accomplished.

Attainable. The goal should be realistic, something that you can accomplish with the time, resources, and effort put into it.

Relevant. The goal is connected to or appropriate for your venture.

Time-Bound. Designate a specific timeframe to achieve the goal.

An example of a S.M.A.R.T. marketing goal for a business is 1,000 new subscribers in the next 12 months. It is **specific** *(1,000 new subscribers)*; **measurable** *(we can easily track the numbers)*; **attainable** *(definitely doable with effort in the designated timeframe)*; **relevant** *(an email list is crucial for any business today)*; and **time-bound** *(the next 12 months)*.

Some common marketing objectives are as follows. You can use these applicable objectives to create your S.M.A.R.T. goals:

- Establish or increase brand exposure and awareness *(this one is usually always relevant)*.

- Increase sales or revenue *(once again, always relevant)*.

- Introduce and promote new products, services, programs.

- Lead generation.

- Expand into new markets or grow market share.

- Grow email list.

- Increase website traffic.

MARKET ANALYSIS & RESEARCH

An analysis of the market involves an in-depth understanding of your target audience, competitors, trends, and economic conditions. This will help you identify possible barriers, reduce or eliminate risks, gauge the market's pulse, and effectively market your products, services, and/or programs.

Target Audience

Majority, if not all, of the research for your target audience was done when you created your avatar in *Chapter 6*, under *Who*. Essentially, you want to know as much as you can about your target audience.

Competitors

You want to research your competitors – who they are, what products, services, and/or programs they offer, the cost, where they are marketing or advertising. Most of this information can be obtained by visiting their website, viewing their marketing materials, and even calling them to inquire. You can start your search using the keywords you've already identified, in the online search engine of your choice.

Trends and Economic Conditions

Here you are looking for specifics on what market and industry trends could impact your progress, as well as what's the overall state of the economy and its impact. Futurist, Faith Popcorn of *BrainReserve*[101] does an amazing job tracking and sharing trends annually that you can capitalize on or avoid.

Economic conditions look at the unemployment levels, inflation, consumer confidence, etc. *The National Bureau of Economic Research*[102] is a great resource to assist you

Take some time to determine what trends and economic conditions are valid for or will have an impact on your venture. Some of this information can also be found in the *SWOT Analysis* you created in *Chapter 6*, under *What*.

MARKETING STRATEGY

Your marketing strategy will provide details for your marketing efforts. It will include your marketing budget, networking, and the five (5) P's: *People, Product, Process, Price,* and *Promotion*.

Marketing Budget

Because marketing is such a huge component of your success, establishing a marketing budget is essential. There are a lot of things you can do for free, but I still recommend that you create a monthly marketing budget to enhance your efforts. This budget will cover expenses like advertising, graphics, print material, video production, photography, website and other technology fees, events, etc. Remember, the less available funds you have, the more effort you must exert. In addition, you must be willing to invest something, even if you must make sacrifices.

Networking

As discussed in the section above, networking must be an important component of your marketing strategy. Please see the system I detailed on page 138 and the template in the *Destiny Starter™ Workbook*.

People

The plan for your life has the potential to be huge; however, the extent to how far you go and the impact that you have – is up to you. Whatever you choose, it is highly likely that you will need a team of people to assist you. Starting out, you may be able to do it all on your own, but at some point, you will need help. You won't be able to do it alone for too long. *(Trust me, I've tried.)*

Effectively leading a team is not easy. I highly recommend that you consider pursuing some form of leadership training. In the book,

Lead Like Jesus, the authors state, "*Try to imagine leaders who lead like Jesus. Leaders who love those they influence so much that they help them get from where they are to where God would have them go. Leaders who hold people accountable, encourage them daily, confront challenges, and bring authenticity, character, and integrity to every interaction. Leaders who want to guide others on the same path. Imagine a world full of those leaders!*"[103]

I can't speak for you, but that's the type of leader I want to be for my team, and I encourage you to give some thought to the type of leader you would like to be.

Throughout the book, we have talked about operating your business in excellence. As the leader, it is important that you define excellence and set the expectation of excellence from your team. It's a conversation you have during the interview process, and one that you frequently have once the team is onboard.

Below we will highlight some options for you to consider when creating your team.

The first thing that you must do is decide exactly what you need help with. Therefore, take some time to think through and write on paper or type what needs to be done, and what qualifications are needed for your new hires. Once you've defined who and what you need, next we will review possible options for acquiring talent.

Working with Freelancers. A significant percentage of the work that needs to be done can be completed using freelancers, like graphic designers, virtual assistants, writers, bloggers, photographers, musicians, interpreters, videographers, contractors, web designers, and other professionals.

FREELANCER AND VIRTUAL ASSISTANT DEFINED

- According to the Freelancer's Union & Upwork, **freelancer** is defined as individuals who perform supplemental, temporary, project- or contract-based work to fully or partially support themselves.[104]

FREELANCER AND VIRTUAL ASSISTANT DEFINED

- According to Investopedia, a **virtual assistant** is an independent contractor who provides administrative services to clients while operating outside of the client's office. A virtual assistant typically operates from a home office but can access the necessary planning documents, such as shared calendars, remotely.[105]

Freelancers are considered independent contractors and not employees of the business. Therefore, they have the freedom to select the projects, days, and times they choose to work.

There are a variety of freelancing websites that provide access to quality freelancers, as well as financial protection for both you and the freelancer. They are structured to hold the funds in an escrow-like account until the project is completed and approved by you before the funds can be released to the freelancer.

You would need to know exactly what you want done, approximately how many hours it will take, and how much you are willing or able to pay. Depending on which platforms you choose, you are able to search for potential freelancers that meet the qualifications of your job or project. Or you can post your job on one or more of the freelance websites and await responses or bids. During your search or as you receive bids from freelancers, you want to see samples and/or review client testimonials from each of them.

To select the appropriate freelancer, pay close attention to their work ethic, communication etiquette, and work quality. Do not make the final payment or release the funds until you've seen and approved the final work. In the event you need to make changes and the freelancer is no longer available, you also want to ask for the editable files (*where possible*). The file format will be .eps, .ai, or .psd. You may not be able to open this file, but a designer can.

You can start your search by typing **find freelancers** in the search engine of your choice. I also provide resources in the *Destiny Starter™ Workbook*.

Small Businesses. If you have access to larger budgets and if you want a little more certainty, I suggest you work with local or online small businesses. You can do an online search or get recommendations from people in your circle. Either way, you want to do your research. As with the freelancers, you want to see samples of their work, review testimonials, and understand the market price for the services you want completed. Caution: Don't pay the full amount upfront; this is a mistake people often make. It is more than reasonable to make a down payment, and then the final payment upon approval or completion of the job.

Employees. If you are not keen on hiring freelancers and outsourcing services, directly hiring employees is your best option. You can choose to hire full- or part-time employees. Keep in mind that there are added costs associated with hiring employees and they include, but are not limited to:

Recruiting	Salary	Taxes
Benefits	Equipment	Space

Also hiring a direct employee introduces a range of legal and financial factors that must be considered. Therefore, it is highly recommended that you converse with a reputable business attorney and/or accountant.

Another option would be working with a temporary staffing agency. Essentially, you hire the agency at a set fee, and the agency hires the worker(s) with your approval and takes responsibility for managing all human resource aspects.

Whichever direction you choose, understand that your team is an invaluable asset. As their leader, you are responsible for establishing the culture and environment they work in. Set appropriate boundaries and take care of them, show them that you value and appreciate them, and they will take good care of you.

Product

By this point, you should have selected your *How*. If not, go back to the *Destiny Starter™ Workbook, Activity 6* and review the organization models discussed there. Remember my recommendation is that you pick one to get started.

Here you want to further develop your product, service, and/or program. If you have a physical product, the product design and packaging may be extremely important. Again, look at the quality and design of *Apple* products. In addition to the focus and care placed in developing cutting-edge technology, they put just as much focus and care on product designs and packaging. If you've purchased an *iPhone, iPad, MacBook*, etc., it looks sleek, feels great in your hand, and it is well packaged in a beautifully designed, yet simple box. In my opinion, nothing compares - it is all done in excellence, as should yours.

Now I get that access to funds may be an issue...but there are viable options like crowdfunding that can help you raise upfront capital. *(See the Destiny Starter™ Workbook for resources.)*

At the end of the day, your product, service, or program must be done in excellence. I highly recommend that you test it out with your family and friends before your official launch. In this test, you want to get honest feedback, what worked, what didn't work, what would they change, what is missing, etc.? Use that feedback to improve the product, service, and/or program. In addition, even after you launch, you still want to get feedback and make the necessary adjustments moving forward.

Process

In alignment with the product section, the process for how the product, service, program is delivered and received needs to be done in excellence as well. Poor processes yield poor results, higher production costs, and poor customer service. Therefore, you want to ensure to have basic standard operating procedures *(SOPs)* for each area outlined below:

Product, Service, or Program Development. How is your product, service, or program produced? What is the process or procedure?

Hiring. What is the hiring process? Do you require resumes? Is a background check necessary? If so, how do you obtain it? How do you market open positions?

Marketing & Promotions. How will you spread the word daily, weekly, monthly, annually, and how will you measure results?

Email Marketing. Today, your email list is definitely linked to your business' financial lifeline. Therefore, it is highly recommended that you create an effective system for managing your email marketing efforts. We talk more about this on pages 153 and 157.

Sales and Distribution. How will your target audience order, request, access, and receive what you have to offer? What is your quality control process?

Accounting. What accounting methods are you using? What software are you using? How do you process payments, refunds, accounts payable, etc.? How often do you reconcile the books?

Customer Service. What are your customer service procedures? How do you handle complaints or mistakes? What type of service can your clients, customers, supporters, or followers expect from you? What's your process for collecting testimonials and constructive feedback?

Reporting. How are you tracking the various components of your business? Like, how many people have purchased a product, service, or program; how many people are following you on social media as opposed to the previous year? What does your financial overview look like?

Price

How are you pricing your product, service, or program? There are several pricing models that you can choose from. Take time to explore them and decide which model will work best for your business. Below, I will highlight five pricing models: freemium, subscription, cost-based, market pricing, and razor & blade.

Freemium. With the freemium pricing model, you give away a portion of, or the complete product, service, or program for free, and you generate revenue via upgrades, advertising, affiliate marketing programs, or some other sources. An example of the freemium pricing model would be the social media management tool, *Hootsuite*. They offer a free plan with limited access to the various tools offered. To take advantage of more, they offer premium monthly plans.

Subscription. With the subscription pricing model, you charge a recurring fee for access to your product, service, or program. The fee can be in any frequency you choose: daily, weekly, monthly, quarterly, semi-annually, annually. An example of the subscription pricing model is *Netflix*. Subscribers pay a monthly fee for unlimited access to all streaming TV shows, movies, documentaries, etc.

Cost-based. With the cost-based pricing model, the price of your product, service, or program is marked up 2–5 times the cost to produce it. Depending on the industry, margins can range from 20%–65% or more. *Apple iPhones* would be an example of a cost-based pricing model. It is estimated that it costs *Apple* anywhere from $350–$450 to manufacture the *iPhone*.[106] They then mark it up and sell it to us for 2–3 times that amount.

Market Pricing. With the market pricing model, the price is based on supply and demand. Think about real estate, the price is contingent upon how much buyers are willing to pay in a given market.

Razor & Blade. The razor & blade pricing model involves a low-priced reusable base item, and a consumable item that must be replaced regularly. Think about inkjet printers...you can purchase an inexpensive printer, but where the manufacturer makes its money is through the repurchase of ink or toner cartridges. The key here is – the printer is useless without the ink or toner.

For additional models, type **pricing models** in the search engine of your choice.

Promotion

How will you let your target audience know you exist? The extent to which you advertise and promote your product, service, or program largely depends on your available time and marketing budget. There are a variety of free and paid options available to you.

Social Media. With or without a budget, you want to aggressively push and grow your social media presence. There is a wide selection of social media platforms – the ones you select will depend on where your target audience is engaging. For instance, *Facebook* may not be the best choice if your target audience is teenagers. According to my goddaughter, *Facebook* is for old people like me. *(I was 41 at the time and didn't realize I was old until she informed me of such.)*

Independent of which platform you choose, you want to ensure that your brand is visible and that there is consistent engagement with your followers. You also want to provide valuable, sharable content. Please note the key here is *valuable content*. You want to deliver content that informs, educates, encourages, inspires, equips, empowers, entertains, etc....it should add value to their lives. In addition, you want to ensure that a call-to- action is included as well (*i.e., visit our website, join our email list, purchase your copy, share your thoughts below, etc.*).

Email List. As mentioned previously, building your email list should be at the top of your marketing plan. The people who opt into your list are those who you must treasure as if your business depended on them – because it does. Therefore, you want to show them that you value and appreciate them by providing valuable content and solutions that help and make their lives better. You don't want to bombard them with spam. Protect the list at all costs, because they are the people who will support what you do and what you put out. So, I repeat, treat them well.

Other Options. If you are in the position where you do have a marketing budget, in addition to social media and email marketing, there is a wide array of other options and some of these are highlighted on the next page.

Take the time to go through the list and select the options that work best for your business. What you want to consider is your business' capacity. Meaning, you and/or your staff can manage it, or you have the funds to pay someone to manage it.

MARKETING IMPLEMENTATION

Once you've thought through and recorded your marketing strategy, next is giving thought to how you will execute that strategy. This includes bringing clarity to who is responsible for each component, structuring your sales funnel(s), defining your email marketing approach, content generation, and sales promotions.

Responsibilities

We talked about this briefly under *Marketing Strategy: People*, but here I would really like you to decide what components of your marketing

PROMOTIONAL OPTIONS		
	ONLINE OPTIONS	OFFLINE OPTIONS
PAID	• Pay-Per-Click Ads • *Google* Ads • *Bing* Ads • *Yahoo* Ads • *Facebook* Ads • *YouTube* Ads • *Instagram* Ads • *Twitter* Ads • Online Radio Ads • Public Relations • Webinars • *Angie's List* • Ads on Popular Blogs • *Hulu* Ads • Digital Magazines and Newspapers	• Local Cable • Public Relations • Offline Media (TV, Radio) • Newspapers • Bulk Mailers • Seminars • Magazines • Door-to-Door Ads • Direct Mailers • Car Signs • Bumper Stickers • Meet and Greets • Launch Parties, Grand Openings • Benches • Taxi Cabs
	ONLINE OPTIONS	OFFLINE OPTIONS
FREE	• *YouTube* • Social Media Channels • Email • Referrals • Your Blog or Guest Blogging • Online Forums or Groups • Press Releases • Online Media • Slideshows • Podcasts • Online Radio • Article Submissions • Newspapers • Crowdfunding • Webinars • *Yelp* • Fundraisers • *Indeed* • Family Friends • SEO • Online Courses • Contests • Surveys • Forums	• Local Posting Boards • Flyers • Word of Mouth • Magazines • Seminars • Newspapers • Press Releases • Offline Media (TV, Radio) • Book Stores Churches, Faith-based Organizations • Fraternities & Sororities • Seminars • Door Stopper Ads • Advertise a Contest • Community Boards • Community Groups • Networking Events

plan you will handle in-house and what will be outsourced. If you are like me, and prefer to do most things yourself, I want to caution you to factor in your available time. Really consider your capacity to execute the components and do them well. Trust me, there will come a time where you simply can't do it all yourself, and you have to find your peace with that.

Sales Funnel

As defined by *InfusionSoft/Keap*, *"a sales funnel is the marketing term for the journey potential customers go through on the way to purchase. There are several steps to a sales funnel, usually known as the top, middle, and bottom of the funnel, although these steps may vary depending on a company's sales model."*[107] Sales funnels work for both online and offline models, and typically has 4–5 levels or steps:

Level 1: Awareness. This level is all about letting your target audience know that you exist, and what you have to offer. Generally, you create awareness by providing useful information that solves a problem. For online ventures, this entails offering free content like blogs, podcasts, *YouTube* videos, etc., that draw awareness to your target audience. For offline ventures, this could entail flyers, posters, newspaper ads, etc. You can find more in the *Promotional Options* table above.

Level 2: Consideration or Interest. On this level you have an opportunity to give your audience a test run of what you have to offer, in exchange for a name, email address, or other contact information. Once you have obtained email addresses and contact information, you can send special discounts and offers to purchase. For online ventures, this could involve free webinars, guides, teleseminars, etc. For offline ventures, it could include product samples, discounts, free delivery, etc.

Level 3: Decision. At this level, the target is ready to buy, and it is crucial to create the best customer experience possible. A positive

SALES FUNNEL

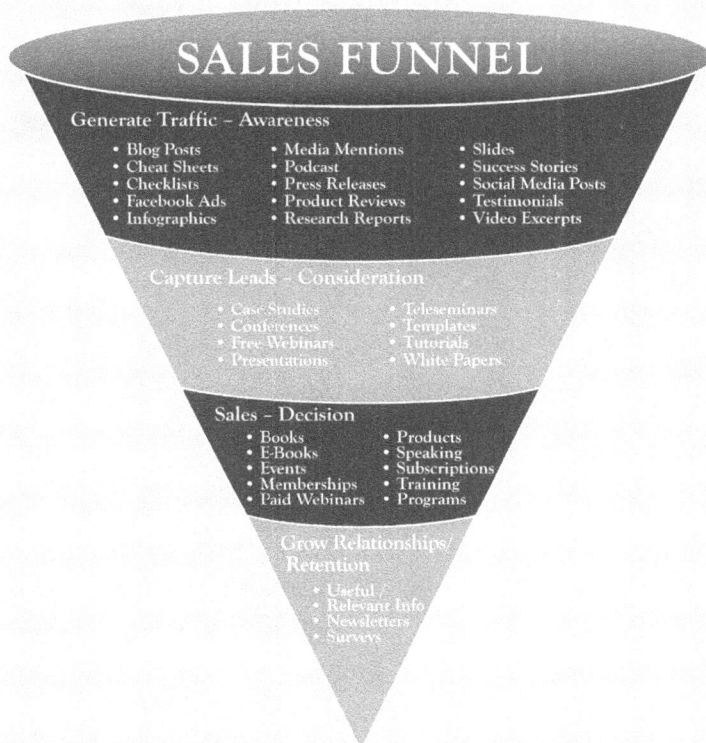

experience can lead to referrals, upsells, and repeat sales. For online ventures, you can offer extras like free shipping to ensure they pull the trigger on the purchase. For offline ventures, you are zooming in on how you treat your customer from the time they enter your space, to the time they exit.

Level 4: Retention. This last level is geared toward retaining the customer. Here you will provide useful, relevant content, product updates, thank yous, etc. You want to keep the customer happy, informed, and engaged.

Depending on the types of products, services, programs, and price levels of what you are offering, you may need multiple sales funnels. In addition, I recommend that your offerings be structured/tiered at various price points. For instance, the *Destiny Starter™* line of products includes the following four (4) tiers with 4 different price points. My goal was to create something to help everyone on whatever level they are on:

- 1st Tier: Book

- 2nd Tier: Digital Course

- 3rd Tier: Live 12-week Training

- 4th Tier: One-on-One Consulting

Email Marketing

I can't say this enough, your email list is an extremely valuable asset. You want to continually be growing this list because it gives you direct access to your audience. Unlike social media or other platforms, it can't be taken away from you. *Facebook* could shut down tomorrow, and all your *Facebook* fans will go with it. Therefore, you want to build a community that you have direct access to.

Here are a couple of simple steps to successfully get you started with your list:

Choose an Email Marketing Platform. It is highly recommended that you don't send blast emails from your personal or business email accounts. They are not set up to effectively manage these types of emails. However, there are several email marketing platforms that are better suited for this task. (*See the Destiny Starter™ Workbook for my recommended resources.*)

Create Your Lead Magnet. A lead magnet is a useful, valuable item that you give away for free, in exchange for an email address and other contact information. It could be e-books, checklists, cheat sheets, reports, templates, etc., or anything you decide that could benefit your audience. For example, one of my lead magnets is the *How to Start a Podcast* tutorial. If your area is financial services, your lead magnet could be something like the *Ten Ways to Invest Your Money in Today's Market*.

Sign-up Forms. Using your email marketing platform, create a sign-up form that you can publish on your website, blogs, and social media. In addition, you can create physical sign-up forms that you use onsite at your store, other locations, and events. If you are a little tech-savvy, you can use platforms that allow you to collect email addresses via text. This is great for speakers, trainers, podcasters, etc. *(See the Destiny Starter™ Workbook for my recommended resources.)*

Automated Emails. When subscribers complete your sign-up form, you want to have a *Welcome* autoresponder in place. Your email marketing platform makes this task rather simple. Essentially, you will write a sincere welcome email that includes the free gift *(lead magnet)* which automatically forwards when someone completes the form. In addition, the email should introduce you and your business, and share a little about how what you offer benefits the subscriber.

Along with the initial automated *Welcome* email, I recommend that you set up at least three (3) additional automated emails that give the subscriber an opportunity to learn more about how what you offer benefits them. These emails should be set up to automatically go out 1/day or 1/week after the initial signup:

Automated Email 2: Testimonials. Here you want to share testimonials from past clients, customers, supporters, and followers. If you don't have testimonials yet, really zoom in on the benefits of your products, services, or programs. In addition, you want to include a special or discounted offer.

Automated Email 3: More Goodies. In this email you will offer another free gift – something of value to the subscriber, and shows how what you offer is the solution to their pain.

Automated Email 4: How Can I or We Help You? This final automated email is an inquiry into how you can help the subscriber. You want to create a short list of questions that you put in survey format using a platform like *Survey Monkey* or *Google Forms*. Possible questions could include, *what would you say is your single biggest challenge or pain right now, or what information would you like to learn more about?* The goal of the survey is to find out specifically how you can help, and then provide the help, if possible.

Lastly, you want to establish a schedule of consistent email engagement. It could be a summary of your weekly or bi-weekly blog, vlog, or podcast posts, with links to the full posts; or it could be a personal story you share; or relevant and useful content. In addition, these subsequent emails should have some type of call-to-action – sign up for a webinar, purchase [product] for 5% off, join us at an upcoming event, etc. Whatever schedule you choose, remember that consistency is key.

Content Generation

Content marketing will most likely play an integral role in your marketing strategy. Whether you are posting on your website, other blogs, social media, podcasting, etc., generating useful, relevant, entertaining, and inspirational content can appeal to current and attract potential clients, customers, supporters, followers.

There are primarily two (2) types of content: original content you create and content you curate. Original content comes in many forms, like cheat sheets, how-to videos, reports, whitepapers, etc. Curated content is that which you find and share. It is essentially other people's content that you believe will be valuable to your audience.

Although original content is best, curated content can also be impactful. You just want to ensure that you utilize it correctly:

- Only share high-quality content that you have fully examined. Meaning, you have read or listened to all of it and know that it will be valuable for your audience.

- Share your opinion or take on the content you are curating. This is easily accomplished by writing a brief blurb about the curated content that you include when shared.

- Give credit to the original creator of the content. You don't want to plagiarize anyone's content, so give credit where credit is due.

- Don't overdo it...ensure that in addition to the curated content, you are creating and sharing original content as well.

Sales Promotions

Sales promotions are special offers pertaining to your products, services, and/or programs that you advertise to your audience. These promotions are usually short-term, temporary specials that you offer to boost sales and attract clients and customers. For instance, *24-Hour Flash Sale: $150 off.*

Monthly, Weekly, and Daily Activities

Next, you want to take the marketing elements you've selected and create a daily, weekly, or monthly schedule that portrays when and what promotions your business will execute. If you take the time to plan it out, it will make things a lot easier and more manageable.

MARKETING ANALYTICS

One of the most important components of your marketing plan is analytics. It's vital that you track what's working and what's not working, based on your *Key Performance Indicators (KPIs)*. The *Alexa* blog defines *KPIs* as *"a metric that demonstrates how effectively you are achieving a key business objective."*[108] Your *KPIs* will vary, depending on what you specifically want to track according to your overall goals and objectives, and they can change over time.

I recommend doing monthly or quarterly analytics. You will use this information to make the necessary adjustments to your marketing strategy.

Majority of the platforms that I recommend in the *Destiny Starter™ Workbook* each provide analytics. In addition, you can use *Google Analytics* to track several *KPIs*.

CUSTOMER SERVICE

The last portion of your marketing that I will talk about here is customer service. Customer service is yet another key component of your strategy. It does no good to implement your strategy, generate viable leads and lose the client, customer, supporter, follower due to poor customer service.

In addition to your customer service SOPs, I recommend that you create a customer service vision statement that you stand on, no matter what. This statement should be short and sweet, based on how you create a positive experience at every customer touchpoint (*wherever your customer finds you*). And it should be shared with your team on a consistent basis. An example customer service vision statement could be *"the customer is always right!"* Once created, this statement should be instrumental in all customer interactions and correspondence.

● ● ●

In closing, I want to stress a couple of key points here:

1. Share the benefits of what you have to offer. Always highlight that you have the solution to your target's pain or problem.

2. Operate in excellence – all the time, every time.

3. Serve people well. Both internal *(team)* and external *(customers, clients, followers, supporters)*.

4. Build an email list.

5. Keep taking action, spreading your message, and moving forward, no matter what! Don't give up!

6. Consistency, consistency, consistency...no matter what you decide to do, commit to being consistent with it.

✎ DESTINY STARTER™ WORKBOOK

See Activity Nine (9) in the *Destiny Starter™ Workbook* to develop all the components discussed here for your simple marketing strategy.

CHAPTER TEN:

FINISH WRITING THE PLAN

All you need is the plan, the road map, and the courage to press on to your destination.[109] – *Earl Nightingale*

Most of the plan has already been created. In this section, you will bring it all together...

WORKING FOR SOMEONE ELSE

COMPLETE THE CAREER ACTION PLAN CANVAS

Your *Career Action Plan* will summarize the components you worked through in this strategy marker. For your convenience, I have created a template in the *Destiny Starter™ Workbook* to help you bring your plan together. It consists of six elements:

Perfect Job/Job Title

- What is your perfect job?
- What is your perfect title?

Job Requirements & Responsibilities

- What are the job requirements for your perfect job?
- What are the job responsibilites for your perfect title?

Career Goals

- Define your long-term goals: 5-10 years out
- Define your short-term goals: 12 months out

Preparation Needs

- Is there anything you need to do to get ready for your perfect job?
- Is there a need for additional trainings or certifications?

Core Compentencies

- What are the qualifications that you have for your perfect job?
- What are the job responsibilites for your perfect title?

Potential Mentors

- Identify individuals who currently have or have previously been in your perfect position.

SAMPLE CAREER ACTION PLAN

Career Action Plan

Date: Version:

Perfect Job/Job Title

Creative Director

Preparation Needs

There are a couple of steps needed to become a Creative Director: 1. Junior Director, 2. Senior Director, 3. Studio Manager, 4. Art Director and 5. Creative Director.

Preparation needs include:
- I love my current employer, and there is a possibility a Creative Director position will open in a couple of years. I want to ensure that I'm ready when that happens.
- Meet with upper management to determine what I need to do to be prepared for that position
- I will set up Google Alerts and Talkwalker Alerts for Senior Director, Studio Manager, Art Director and Creative Director jobs.

Core Competencies

- Adobe Creative Suite/Software Efficient
- Excellent Communication Skills
- Basic HTML Knowledge
- Typography
- Print Design
- Problem Solving

Job Requirements & Responsibilities

Responsibilities
- Initiate and design complex and simple marketing plans based on client specifications
- Ensure that each project has the specific financial and personnel resources it requires to be successful
- Attend sales presentations to help clients understand the creative angle of each marketing program
- Work with the executive team to implement marketing materials for the firm to help increase the firm's exposure
- Collaborate with design personnel to ensure that all creative ideas are presented properly

Requirements
- Bachelor's Degree in Marketing required (Master's Degree preferred)
- 5+ years' experience in a marketing leadership role
- Proven success in managing marketing teams
- Portfolio of previous work that displays an ability to turn an idea into a visual piece
- Strong communication and computer skills
- Experience with Adobe Creative Suite a plus
- Comprehensive knowledge of the marketing design process

Potential Mentors

- Jacob Case, Just Creative
- Michael Bierut, Pentagram
- Kate Moross, Studio Moross
- Rafael Smith, Ideo.org
- Gail Anderson, Anderson Newton Design

Career Goals *(Add Target Dates)*

Long-Term Goals *(5-10 Years Out)*
- Obtain Adobe Certified Expert Certifications with Adobe Photoshop, Illustrator and InDesign (December 2023)
- Complete the John Maxwell Leadership Certification (December 2024)
- Secure a marketing leadership role (December 2025)
- Earn $150-200K annually

Short-Term Goals *(12-Months Out)*
- Secure senior graphic designer position (December 2021)
- Continue to build my portfolio (Monthly)
- Finish online coding course (June 2021)
- Take color theory course (October 2021)
- Attend the 2020 AIGA Design Conference (November 2021)

www.begreatglobal.com

BE GREAT

WORKING FOR YOURSELF

COMPLETE THE BUSINESS MODEL CANVAS

Here we will use *The Business Model Canvas*[110] to bring all of the components you worked through in this strategy marker. This 1-page business plan is a strategic management and organizational tool that allows you to describe, sketch, design, challenge, and invent your organization model. The canvas is composed of nine elements:

Customer Segments

- For whom are we creating value?
- Who are our most important customers?

Types
- Mass Market
- Niche Market
- Segmented
- Diversified
- Multi-sided Platform

Value Propositions

- What value do we deliver to the customer?
- Which one of our customer's problems are we helping to solve?
- What bundles of products and services are we offering to each Customer Segment?
- Which customer needs are we satisfying?

Characteristics
- Newness — Price
- Performance — Cost Reduction
- Customization — Risk Reduction
- "Getting the Job Done" — Accessibility
- Convenience/Usability — Design
- Brand/Status

Channels

- Through which Channels do our Customer Segments want to be reached?
- How are we reaching them now?
- How are our Channels integrated?
- Which ones work best?
- Which ones are most cost-efficient?
- How are we integrating them with customer routines?

Channel Phases
- **Awareness.** How do we raise awareness?
- **Evaluation.** How do we help customers evaluate our organization's Value Proposition?
- **Purchase.** How do customers purchase?
- **Delivery.** How do we deliver a Value Proposition?

Customer Relationships

- What type of relationship does each of our Customer Segments expect us to establish and maintain with them?
- Which ones have we established?
- How are they integrated with the rest of our business model?
- How costly are they?

Examples
- Personal Assistance
- Dedicated Personal Assistance
- Self-Service
- Automated Services
- Communities

Revenue Streams 💰

- For what value are our customers willing to pay?
- For what do they currently pay?
- How are they currently paying?
- How would they prefer to pay?
- How much does each Revenue Stream contribute to overall revenues?

Types	Fixed-Pricing	Dynamic Pricing
- Asset sale	- List Price	- Negotiation (Bargaining)
- Usage Fees	- Product Dependent	- Yield Management
- Subscription Fees	- Customer Segment Dependent	- Real-time-Market
- Lending	- Volume Dependent	
- Renting		
- Leasing		
- Licensing		
- Brokerage Fees		

Key Activities ✓

- What Key Activities do our Value Propositions require?
- Our Distribution Channels?
- Customer Relationships?
- Revenue Streams?

Categories
- Production
- Problem Solving
- Platform/Network

Key Resources 👨‍🏭

- What Key Resources do our Value Propositions require?
- Our Distribution Channels?
- Customer Relationships?
- Revenue Streams?

Types of Resources
- Physical
- Intellectual (brand patents, copyrights, data)
- Human
- Financial

Key Partners 🔗

- Who are our Key Partners?
- Who are our Key Suppliers?
- Which Key Resources are we acquiring from partners?
- Which Key Activities do partners perform?

Motivation for Partnerships
- Optimization and economy
- Reduction of risk and uncertainty
- Acquisition of particular resources and activities

Cost Structure 🏷️

- What are the most important costs inherent in our business model?
- Which Key Resources are most expensive?
- Which Key Activities are most expensive?
- Is the business cost-driven or value-driven?

Sample Characteristics
- Fixed Costs (salaries, rents, utilities)
- Variable Costs
- Economies of Scale
- Economies of Scope

SAMPLE BUSINESS MODEL CANVAS

The Business Model Canvas

Designed for: Anita Clinton Enterprises, LLC   Designed by: Anita Clinton   Date: 2019   Version: 1

Key Partners

- Strategic Alliances - seasoned experts in their fields who provide programs, resources, services, and training for clients
- SBA/Score
- Entrepreneurial Centers
- Business Consultants and Coaches
- Speaking Bureaus
- Conference Planners/Hosts

Venues
- Faith- and Community-based Organizations
- Civic and Social Groups
- Professional and Business Associations

Key Activities

- Speaking
- Consulting
- Writing/Publishing
- Training
- Podcast
- Resources - content creation and curation

Key Resources

- Intellectual Property - internal and external
- Data and Analytics
- Platforms:
  - Webhosting Services
  - Social Media Platforms
  - Podcast Hosting
  - Wordpress Platform
  - Online Teaching Platform
  - Product/Merchandise Fulfillment
  - Email Marketing Platform(s)
  - Online Payment System(s)
  - Print-on-Demand Platform(s)

Value Propositions

Unique Value Proposition
We take the worry out of you not knowing the call on your life, the anxiety out of how to do what you've been called to do, and the fear of doing it all alone.

Unique Selling Proposition
We help DREAMERS use their Superpower to live an extraordinary life and transform the face of the world, using the 45-day, 2 hours a day Destiny Starter RoadMap.

Customer Relationships

- Assistance/Guidance
- On-Demand Products/Resources
- Communities of Like-Minded Individuals
- Networking and Collaborative Opportunities
- Support and Accountability

Channels

- Website
- Podcast
- Social Media
- Word of Mouth
- Blogs
- Conferences and Live Events

Customer Segments

Dreamers in search of happiness, fulfillment, and money...

"It's time you make a living doing work you actually LOVE!"

Dreamers
- Age: 25-54
- Economic Level: Middle to upper class (lives in the city or surburbs)
- Annual Income: >$45,000
- Sex: Male/Female
- Education: High School diploma and/or some degree of higher education
- Values: Faith, Authenticity, Integrity, Determination, Responsibility, Trustworthiness, and Knowledge-Seeking

Event Hosts

* Middle-Class Salaries = $45,200-$135,600
* Upper Class = $136,000+
Source: Pew 2016.

Cost Structure

Platform Fees
- Paypal, Square, and Stripe Fees
- Webhosting Fees
- Podcast Hosting Fees
- Merchandising & Product Fulfillment Fees
- Mailchimp/Kajabi/Thinkific Fees

Other Fees
- Advertising and Marketing Costs
- Office Supplies
- Rent Fees
- Association Dues
- Subscription Fees
- Non-reimbursable Travel and Lodging Fees

Revenue Streams

- Training Programs
  - Digital Courses: $69-$299
  - Live Online Trainings: $299-$1,999
  - Live Onsite Trainings: $5,000+
- Affiliate Marketing: Varies
- Books/Product Sales: $15-$75
- Merchandising: $15-$50

ThinkPod/Mastermind Groups: $299
Speaking Engagements: $300-$10,000
Consulting Services: $225/hr

Strategyzer
strategyzer.com

✎ DESTINY STARTER™ WORKBOOK

See Activity Ten (10) in the *Destiny Starter™ Workbook* to compose either your career plan, using the available template, or one-page business plan, using the *Strategyzer* template *(see sample on next page).*

BRINGING IT ALL TOGETHER

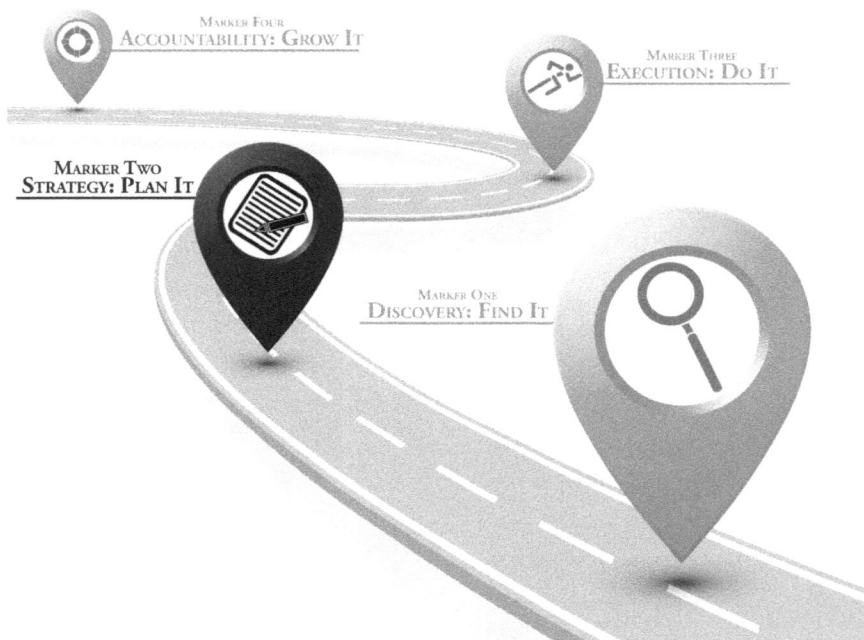

A s we conclude *Marker Two – Strategy: Plan It* of the *Destiny Starter™ RoadMap*, let's review...

We divided this section into two parts: *Part One: Let's Talk About You* and *Part Two: Now, Let's Talk About Your Vision*. In the first part, we dived into the importance of working beyond the pain(s) and emotional baggage of your past, and renewing your mind, body, and soul.

In the second part, we dealt with the specifics of the *Call* on your life. We pinpointed your vision; defined your *Who, Why, What, How, Where,* and *When*; created your personal and/or business brand;

devised a simple marketing plan; and developed your career action plan or one-page business plan;.

You have achieved a lot in this section of the book. Next, we will be talking about *Execution*, actually playing the game of your life.

For now, let's celebrate the completion of *Marker Two – Strategy*.

Kudos to you! Go ahead exhale and smile because the planning part is over.

From My Heart to Yours

I AM IS ALL YOU NEED

There's a familiar biblical story that speaks about the *Purpose* and *Call* on the life of Moses. Moses was born in Egypt at a time when Pharaoh, the King, had commanded that all Hebrew boys be killed as soon as they were born.

Moses' mother sought to save him and decided to place Moses in a basket along the edge of the Nile River. Pharaoh's daughter rescued and raised him as her own.

Fast forward to years later, grown Moses witnessed an Egyptian beating a Hebrew slave, and Moses stepped in, killing the Egyptian. As the news spread to Pharaoh, he immediately put out an APB for Moses – who then fled to the land of Midian.

Approximately 40 years later...here is Moses living comfortably in his new life and God Calls. He tells Moses that he will lead the Israelites out of bondage in Egypt to Canaan, a land flowing with milk and honey. So as Moses starts to process all of this – he realizes just how big a task this would be.

You see, we are talking about Moses leading 1 million plus people out of the hands of Pharaoh, the almighty ruler of that time, from the place that had his image carved on one of *Egypt's Most Wanted* stones. Really!!!

So, what does Moses do? Like most of us, he begins making up excuses why he can't do this. *"Lord, I can't do this – it is too big for me, these people won't trust or believe in me, my skin's the wrong color, I don't have enough money or resources, the timing just isn't right – I will be more prepared when I [you fill in the blank]. God, isn't there someone else You could send who is more qualified or who can actually pull this thing off? I simply can't do this by myself."*

And just as God responded to Moses, He is saying to you, *"I AM THAT I AM."* In other words, *"I AM"* all that you need to do what I have Called you to do. You don't need an Aaron, you don't need a Suze Orman, a Dr. Phil or even an Oprah Winfrey to open the door. Independent of how much money you do or don't have, how much scholastic education you have or haven't obtained, how well you do or don't speak, even whether the color of your skin does or doesn't match theirs, I AM has sent you and I AM will open every door; I AM will break down every barrier in place to hinder you. So, stop making excuses, stop trying to help Him out and just trust and believe that I AM has your back, and I AM is all that you need.

– Anita "AC" Clinton

Marker Three

Execution: Do It

OVERVIEW

DO IT

Hard work pays off – hard work beats talent any day, but if you're talented and work hard, it's hard to be beat.[111] *–Robert Griffin, III*

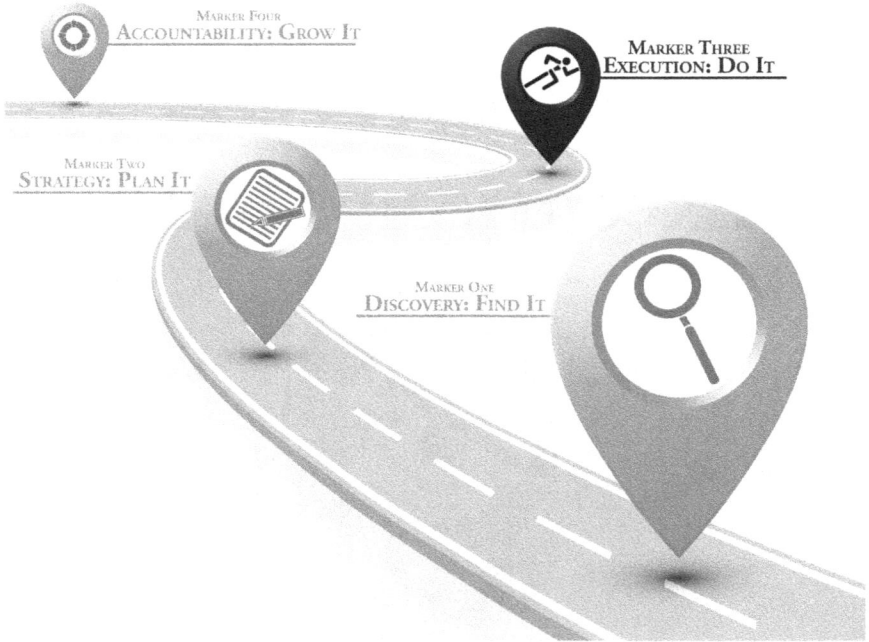

We are officially at the third marker of the *Destiny Starter™ RoadMap* called *Execution: Do It*. You have no idea how ecstatic I am for you in this moment. You are so close to walking boldly in your *Greatness*, but for that to happen you must get on the court to play the game. This is not just any game; it is the game of your life. It won't be easy, but trust me, it is an amazing game to play!!!

So, if you are ready, let's hop right in...*come on, let's do this!*

CHAPTER ELEVEN

CAN YOU SEE IT?

You were born to win, but to be a winner, you must plan to win, prepare to win, and expect to win.[112] *– Zig Ziglar*

L eadership expert, John Maxwell, stated in his book, *Your Road Map for Success,* "*German poet and novelist Johann Wolfgang von Goethe once said, 'Thinking is easy, acting is difficult, and to put one's thoughts into action is the most difficult thing in the world.' Maybe that's why so few people follow through and act on their goals. According to Gregg Harris, two-thirds of people surveyed (sixty-seven of one hundred) set goals for themselves. But of those sixty-seven, only ten have made realistic plans to reach their goals. And out of those ten, only two follow through and actually make them happen.*"[113]

Think about the reality of that, they started with surveying one hundred (100) people. Of those one hundred (100), sixty-seven (67) of them set goals. Of the sixty-seven (67) that set goals, only ten (10) created action plans to achieve the goals set. Of the ten (10) that created the actions plans, only two (2) made the goals a reality. That's two (2) out of one hundred (100) people who actually achieved their goals.

For someone like me, those numbers are alarming. And they support my view on why writing goals and executing an action plan to achieve them are vital. Therefore, your success or failure may very well be contingent upon this. So, I encourage you to take this seriously and don't skip over this section.

Here we will discuss what I'm calling the *Destiny Board,* also known as a *vision board.* Your *Destiny Board* represents (*via images*) what you want to do, who you want to be, and whatever it is that you desire.

It will consist of pictures, phrases, keywords, etc. Use the instructions below to create your *Destiny Board*. This is intended to be simple and you should have fun creating it. In fact, I encourage you to get the entire family involved to create both individual and family goals. So, let's go!

DESTINY BOARD: OUTLINE

The first step in preparation for creating your *Destiny Board* is to develop an outline. This outline will help you gather your thoughts and lay the foundation for the board. I encourage you to review and update this outline at a minimum of once a year. When you review it, you will be surprised at exactly what you have accomplished and how your life has changed. Use the template in the *Destiny Starter™ Workbook* to draft your outline, and the instructions below:

Section 1 – Define Ten Power-Packed Action Words

List ten positive action words that describe you presently and/or the person you will become walking inside your *Calling*. Use a dictionary or thesaurus if necessary (*i.e. hardworking, determined, responsible, etc.*).

Section 2 – Define Ten Words of Affirmation for You & Your Call

Words of affirmation are positive words and sayings that vividly describe what and who you are presently or want to be in the near future. You can be as creative as you like, and you can also use biblical references for your affirmations. I challenge you to get bold with your words of affirmation (*i.e. I am a New York Times Best-selling Author*).

Section 3 – Rewrite Your zog Statement

We've already created your ZOG *Statement* in *Chapter 3*.

Section 4 – Define 1-5 Long-Term Goals

Write your S.M.A.R.T. long-term goals, detailing exactly what you would like to accomplish in the next 5-10 years. S.M.A.R.T goals are specific, measurable, attainable, relevant, and time-bound (*see breakdown on pages 90 & 142*). I encourage you to go way out there – remember, no limits or boundaries. These goals should be big and possibly extend far beyond your current capabilities (*i.e. I will discover the cure for HIV/AIDS*).

Section 5 – Define Specific Short-Term Goals

Write your S.M.A.R.T. short-term goals defining what you want to accomplish within the next twelve months. The outline is setup for you to define your goals in six (6) areas of your life: Relationship, Money, Business/Career, Health & Wellness, Spiritual Development, and Personal Development. Therefore, your can establish short-term goals in all six (6) areas, or only the areas of your choice. (*Note: For the purposes of this book, at the minimum, you want to establish goals for the Money & Business/Career sections.*) It is important that you be extremely specific with these goals. Once you've defined the goals, next you want to create the steps or actions necessary to achieve the goals. And, lastly, each goal should have a target deadline when you want the goal to come to fruition. They each should be a stepping stone to get you to the vision above. (*See the sample outline on next page.*)

PREPARATION FOR THE DESTINY BOARD

Now that you have your outline, let's keep it moving. The next step is gathering your supplies:

- Poster board, scrapbook, or three-ring binder with blank pages.

DESTINY STARTER™ – CAN YOU SEE IT?

SAMPLE DESTINY BOARD OUTLINE			
SECTION 1 – DESCRIPTIVE WORDS			
• Approachable	• Determined	• Happy	• Hardworking
• Kind	• Punctual	• Talented	• Wealthy

SECTION 2 – WORDS OF AFFIRMATION

- I am beautifully, fearfully and wonderfully made
- I am Kingdom-minded and focused on serving others
- I am walking in my purpose
- I am like a tree planted by the rivers of water, producing an abundance of fruit
- I am prospering in good health, even as my soul prospers

SECTION 3 – ZOG STATEMENT

To physically, economically, and spiritually change the lives of others through empowerment and strategic community planning/development, while creating wealth for my family that can be passed down from generation to generation.

SECTION 4 – LONG-TERM GOALS (5-10 YEARS)

1. Be featured in and on the cover of Black Enterprise and Inc. Magazines
2. Rebuild desolate communities physically, economically, and spiritually
3. Invest in profitable businesses and revitalize failing businesses that have potential for success
4. Purchase a home for my mother, and my dream home and cars (including the Bentley Continental GT)
5. Donate annually $1 million to my pastor's mission and $1 million to St. Jude Medical Center

SECTION 5 – SHORT-TERM TARGET GOALS & ACTIONS (12-MONTHS)

Cat.	Goal	Steps/Action	Target Date
Relationships	Establish Work/Life Balance	Do something fun outside of work	Monthly
		Visit and spend quality time with family	Monthly
		Attend a social event/gathering	Quarterly
		Take a getaway to rest and relax	August
Finances	Grow Savings and Increase All Three Credit Scores Over 700	Update Financial Tracker for the current year and consistently utilize it to manage finances	Saturdays: Bi-Weekly
		Continue to pay bills on time and pay all credit balances to $0 each month	Saturdays: Bi-Weekly
		Deposit a minimum of $500 per month in savings	Monthly
Business/ Career	Write and Publish 1st Book	Create outline	January 15
		Write 2 Chapters per week	August 1
		Finalize Editing	September 15
		Send to Printer	October 10
		Official Book Release	December 1
Health & Wellness	Drop/Maintain Weight Under 200lbs	Work out consistently 4 times a week	Weekly
		Eat 3 healthy, nutritious meals and 2 snacks a day	Daily
		Drink 64 ounces of water daily	Daily
		Fast between 7pm – 7am	Daily
Spiritual Development	Strengthen Relationship with God	Consistently pray and meditate/study daily	Daily/Weekly
		Read through the Bible from beginning to end	December 31
		Attend Bible study	Every Wednesday
Personal Development	Increase Knowledge	Read an educational, informative and/or empowering book	Monthly
		Attend 2 business conferences	Semi-Annually
		Hire a Mentor/Coach	March 31

- Magazines – compile a stack of different magazines. You will use the magazines to pull images for your board. You can also find images in newspapers and on the internet. Be creative!

- Glue or tape and scissors.

- A variety of photos of yourself in different poses, close-ups, etc. If you don't have pictures readily available, have a friend or relative take them using a cell phone. You can upload them to the computer and print them on your printer or go to Walgreens and have them printed.

- Pens, markers, crayons (depending on how you want the overall board to look).

Each section of your outline will be used to develop your *Destiny Board*. The format of your *Destiny Board* will vary, depending on if you are using a poster board, scrapbook, or three-ring binder.

POSTER BOARD

If you are using a poster board, adhere to the following steps:

- Pinpoint a picture that you love and speaks to your *Call*. It can be a picture of you, your product, or something that represents your service or program. Place that picture in the center of your board and add one of your descriptive words or words of affirmation under or above the picture.

- Add your ZOG *Statement* at the very top or bottom of your board.

- Look through the magazines or images that you have and find pictures that depict your long-term goals. Once you identify them, start placing them loosely on the board. Glue or tape them once you've determined the placement for each.

- In addition to adding the images, you want to add more of the descriptive words or words of affirmation on the board. You can also add the exact goals that you wrote in *Section 4*.

- If there is space available, you can repeat the previous steps for your short-term goals.

You can make your board aesthetically pleasing by adding designs, glitter, paint, etc. You could also use artistic edged scissors for decorative detailing on images. Be as creative or not as you like.

SAMPLE DESTINY BOARD

Source: Dorothy-Inez Del Tufo, www.dorothyinez.com.

SCRAPBOOK OR 3-RING BINDER

If you are using a scrapbook or three-ring binder, follow these steps:

- Pinpoint a picture that you love and speaks to your *Call*. It can be a picture of you, your product, or something that represents your service or program. The image should really speak to you. Place that picture in the center of the first page and add one of your descriptive words or words of affirmation under or above the picture.

- Add your ZOG *Statement* in the middle of page 2.

- Look through the magazines and images that you have and find pictures that depict your long-term goals. Once you identify them, start placing them on the subsequent pages of the book.

- In addition to adding the images, you want to add more of the descriptive words or words of affirmation on the pages. You can also add the exact goals that you wrote in *Section 4*.

- Repeat previous steps for short-term goals.

- Once again, you can make your book aesthetically pleasing by adding designs, glitter, paint, etc. You could also use artistic edged scissors for decorative detailing on images. Be as creative or not as you like.

DESTINY BOARD: WHAT'S NEXT?

Once you finish the *Destiny Board*, you want to place it somewhere you can see it daily. In fact, make it a priority to view and update it frequently. An easy way to do this is to view the *Destiny Board* before you go to sleep at night and/or when you get up in the morning. You want the images and words implanted in your mind. The ultimate goal is to create a visual of where you are going that you can look at frequently until manifestation. It becomes a visual part of your personal commercial.

✎ DESTINY STARTER™ WORKBOOK

See Activity Eleven (11) in the *Destiny Starter™ Workbook* to compose your *Destiny Board Outline.* (*Note: I also use a similar outline to set my goals each year. I provide the link to the goals template in the Destiny Starter™ Workbook.*)

CHAPTER TWELVE:

FAITH TO DO THE IMPOSSIBLE

Faith is to believe what you do not see; the reward of this faith is to see what you believe.[114]
– Saint Augustine

T he way I visualize the *Destiny Path* is through the image of a bridge. At any bridge, there are usually two sides divided by a huge body of water. At this point in your journey, you are literally standing on one side of the land and your *Call* is just across the huge body of water. The only obstacle is that once you get to this point, the bridge doesn't exist and the only way to cross over to the other side is by faith and action.

I have been a huge fan of the cartoon, *X-men*, since I was a kid. So, when the movies came out, I was ecstatic to see each of them and they did not disappoint. There is a scene in one of the movies where *Magneto (the mutant that has the ability to control and manipulate metal)* is walking across thin air. However, as he walks, a large bridge of metal tiles literally assembles themselves under his feet. I call them the tiles of provision.

This is how I envision the bridge being built as we move forward in faith across the huge body of water. When we make the first step, the tiles of provision are being assembled under our feet. When we stop moving, they stop assembling, if we go back, the tiles ahead of us disappear, when we begin moving forward, they start back assembling again. It is through faith and action that you build the bridge that gives you access to the other side, known as your *Call*.

FAITH NEVER MAKES SENSE

Bill Winston, my former pastor, would constantly remind us that *faith doesn't make sense; it makes faith.* When you get to this point on your *Destiny Path*, faith is the end-all and be-all.

Oh my, this is way outside of Anita's comfort zone. I am a very analytical person, and huge on logical thinking and reasoning. However, when walking in faith, all of that has to go out of the window. I've found that if I'm going to operate in faith, there is no reasoning – most of the time it simply doesn't make sense. Therefore, I'm learning not to even try and figure out how the tiles are laid, but just to walk and trust that they will be provided. I am amazed all the time with how things just seem to fall perfectly into place, and it makes no logical sense how it happens.

So, if you are the type of person that seeks control *(like me)*, then you must get comfortable with letting go or being willing to be uncomfortable and still let it go. Believe me, it is not the easiest thing to do, but it is necessary if you choose to go far and beyond in your *Call.*

Now don't misunderstand what I'm saying here; I'm not saying that you shouldn't have a plan, but with the plan in hand, you must be willing to step out there in faith, believing that this thing is possible, even if it doesn't make sense.

SHATTERING IMPOSSIBILITIES

One Sunday morning, I decided to visit the church home of an associate. I had met the pastor of the church at a planning meeting, and was given an invitation to attend their church. I arrived at the church early and as I walked into the sanctuary, the banner on the front wall caught my eye. It read, *Shattering Impossibilities.*

As I found my seat and waited for the service to begin, I could not take my eyes off the banner. After meditating on the words – I begin to think about boundaries. I begin to question, why we establish boundaries for what we can and cannot accomplish. It is remarkably interesting to me how often we limit ourselves. We create impossibilities in our lives.

If you don't get anything else from reading this book, get this, **the only limits that are in play in your life are the limits that you set.** We are capable of doing amazing things, and the only prerequisite is that we believe.

No matter what anyone tells you, no matter what others have or have not done or been able to do, when it comes to the *Call* on your life as defined in this book, you are able to achieve anything that you believe is possible for you.

There are many examples of people who have achieved what others thought was impossible. Let's take a look at a few of those examples here:

Cliff Young[115]

Cliff Young was a 61-year-old Australian farmer who in 1983 entered and won the *Sydney to Melbourne Ultramarathon*. The marathon is an annual, 544 miles *(875 kilometers)*, 7-day race that athletes trained to run 18 hours a day, and sleep for 6 hours. But not Young; he showed up at the race wearing overalls and boots, ran 24 hours straight for 5 days, and finished in first place. Young was unaware of the norms *(or limitations)* that had been established for the race, and he simply believed that he could complete the race in overalls and boots. And guess what, he did it!

DESTINY STARTER™ – FAITH TO DO THE IMPOSSIBLE

Chris Gardner[116]

Chris Gardner is the founder of *Gardner Rich & Co.*, a multi-million-dollar investment firm. He grew up in a dysfunctional family, he was physically abused by his stepfather, and he and his siblings were in and out of the foster care system. At the age of eight, his mother was imprisoned for the attempted murder of her husband. Although absent for most of his life, Gardner's mother instilled in him the concept of *self-reliance*. She told him that if he wanted something to happen in his life, it was totally up to him. As he became an adult, he had many setbacks, but he was determined to succeed in life.

Like me, you, too, have probably seen the movie about Gardner's life called, *"The Pursuit of Happyness"* released by *Columbia Pictures* in December 2006. In the movie, we see that his life changed drastically when he witnessed a well-dressed man exiting a red Ferrari. *(Note: he started with a vision, the red Ferrari.)*

Gardner approached the man and inquired what he did for a living. The man advised that he was a stockbroker and Gardner's mental wheels started spinning. Against all odds – dealing with divorce, raising his young son alone, becoming broke and homeless, even spending time in jail – Gardner pushed through it all to become a self-made millionaire. He was able to achieve the success and reach heights that no one in his family or inner circle was able to achieve. He did the impossible through determination and the drive to succeed at all costs.

President Barack Obama

President Barack Obama is an African man who was abandoned by his father and raised by his Caucasian grandparents with very little connection and interaction with people that looked like him. However, in spite of the barriers that he had to overcome growing up, his tenacity and will to make a difference in the lives of others (*can we say Purpose*) took him to the highest office in the free world, the *United States' Presidency*. He was able to achieve something that no other African American man has achieved thus far. During his candidacy, he was able to unite hundreds of thousands of people across the world who were supporting him, a black man. Talk about the impossible being possible!

Susan Boyle[117]

Susan Boyle is a talented singer who did not meet the industry's standard for the average professional singer. This little 48-year-old woman came on the scene to audition for a talent contest and stated that she had a dream to be a professional singer. Amid the really – *you must be kidding me* stares and people laughing in her face, she opened her mouth and WHAT!!! Her debut album sold over 700,000 copies in the first week and has sold millions of copies thereafter. She has been nominated for several Grammy awards with the likes of Justin Beiber, Lady Gaga, John Mayer, and Katy Perry. Talk about shattering *unrealistic dreams*!

Michael Jordan[118]

Michael Jordan is one of, if not, the greatest basketball player of all times. In his early years, Michael Jordan was cut from his high school basketball team. However, instead of giving up, he decided to work on his game. Jordan is quoted saying, *"Whenever I was working out and got tired and figured I ought to stop, I'd close my eyes and see that list in the locker room without my name on it."*

Essentially, he made up his mind that failure was not an option. And with persistence and perseverance, Michael Jordan achieved the impossible. He played 15 seasons in the *NBA*, received *5 MVP awards, 10 All-NBA First Team* designations, *9 All-Defensive First Team* honors, *14 NBA All-Star Game* appearances, *3 All-Star MVP* awards, 10 scoring titles, 3 steel titles, 6 *NBA Finals MVP Awards*, and the 1988 *NBA Defensive Player of the Year Award*. He was named the greatest *North American Athlete of the 20th Century*, and he is a two-time inductee in the *Basketball Hall of Fame*.

Mary Kay Ash[119]

Mary Kay Ash is the founder of the widely successful cosmetics company, *Mary Kay Cosmetics, Inc.* She launched her dream in 1963 with a $5,000 investment. From there, she built a global independent sales force with over 3 million women. According to her bio, she is recognized as America's greatest woman entrepreneur who stood her own in a man's world, blazing the path for women.

In her business, she adopted the *Golden Rule* as her guiding philosophy, determining that the best course of action in virtually any situation could be easily discerned by doing unto others as you would have them do unto you. She also steadfastly believed that life's priorities should be kept in their proper order, which to her meant putting faith first, family second, and career third.

She has received a number of prestigious awards, including: *100 Greatest Women of 100 Years* by the *YWCA of Metropolitan Dallas*; *A&E Television* produced *Mary Kay* which aired on the *Biography Channel*; PBS and the *Wharton School of Business' 25 Most Influential Business Leaders of the Last 25 Years*; *Baylor University's Greatest Female Entrepreneur in American History*; *Most Outstanding Woman in Business in the 20th Century, Lifetime Television*; *National Business Hall of Fame, Fortune*; *Pathfinder Award, National Association of Women Business Owners*; one of *America's 25 Most Influential Women, The World Almanac and Book of Facts*; and *Horatio Alger Distinguished American Citizen Award*. Impossible or I'm Possible!

With that being said, you can't tell me that **unrealistic dreams** are unattainable. I believe we all were created for *Greatness* and that the only limits and boundaries that exist in each of our lives are those that we set for ourselves. We can go as far as we choose, or not, based on what we **believe is possible** in our lives. The key here is, you have to believe in you, even if no one else does.

In my personal life, I've always had the attitude that I could do whatever I set my mind to. Growing up, my family spoiled me to the extent that I just didn't understand the word no.

I was accustomed to getting my way in all circumstances. So, with the mindset that no didn't apply to me - my belief system (*subconscious*) was already programmed that I could do whatever I set my mind to.

Up until this point in my life, I have accomplished more than anyone in my family, even if I include my setbacks. When people told me I couldn't do this or that, I was determined to prove them wrong. I've had many ups and downs - but at the end of the day, I have achieved what I said I would and will continue to move forward with that mindset. In my mind, *failure is not an option* - after all, you only fail in life if you quit.

So, when my long-term vision includes creating generational wealth and being in the position to fund and invest in businesses, real estate, and other investment ventures - it is as good as done. It doesn't matter that no one in my family has been able to do this, no one in my inner circle has achieved results to this magnitude, or even the fact that things didn't work out as planned in my earlier attempts. I am destined for success and not only do I believe it is possible for me, I know it is waiting on me to show up. Period!

I encourage you, this day, to adopt the same attitude and let's reach new heights together. I was told once that *it is lonely at the top* –

simply because very few actually make it there!!! Together, let's change that...

DON'T EXPECT IT TO BE EASY

There is nothing like walking boldly into your *Call*; however, it's typically not going to be a walk in the park. As I mentioned previously, the task, the assignment won't be a challenge for you, but everything else has the potential to be challenging.

As T.D. Jakes states in his book, *Crushing*, *"Every person of destiny will become familiar with pain."*[120] It will hit you when you least expect it. However, you can't quit. In those times, your *Why* must remain front and center, because people are depending on you.

In her book, *Hello, Tomorrow!*, Cindy Trimm writes, *"Don't quit, make course-corrections as needed so that your ship arrives at its destination at the appointed time."*[121] Course-corrections are not only necessary, but vital on your *Destiny Path*.

COURSE-CORRECTION EXAMPLE: THE EREBUS STORY[122]

On November 28, 1979, *Air New Zealand Flight 901*, in route to Antarctica crashed into the *Mt. Erebus* volcano, killing the 257 passengers onboard. The much sought-after flights to Antarctica had started 18-months earlier. During a technology upgrade, a data entry operator mistakenly keyed a 4 instead of a 6 into the system that produced the airline's flight plans.

This 2-degree difference would shift the plane's route nearly 30 miles West, and the error went unnoticed for 14 months. Then, the night before *Flight 901* took off, the flight planners decided to make a small course-correction that when coupled with the 2-degree data error (*made 14 months earlier*), unknowingly largely impacted the flight's path – guiding it directly into the Mt. Erebus volcano. These two seemingly minor course-corrections resulted in the death of 257 passengers.

This is definitely a sad story, but the point I'm trying to make here is that small course-corrections can largely impact outcomes. As such, on your *Destiny Path*, you must be flexible and willing to course-correct along the way to ensure that you remain locked on your destination.

BUSY-NESS VS PRODUCTIVITY

Be on the lookout for feelings of overwhelm and frustration by the task at hand, called *busy-ness*. You must recognize this as a distraction and understand that there is a difference between being busy and being productive. You can get to the point where you are extremely busy, but not much is actually getting done.

BUSY-NESS & PRODUCTIVITY DEFINED[123]

According to *Webster*, **busy** is defined as:
- full of activity
- cluttered with detail to the point of being distracted

On the contrary, **productivity** is defined as:
- creating by physical or mental effort
- bring into existence; giving rise to; causing

The time and effort that you put into the *Call* should be defined, organized, and most importantly, produce results.

Operating within your *Zone of Greatness*, performing the necessary task to be who you are *Called* to be, should be second nature. Should there be any struggle, any opposition – it will come from outside forces and not your inability to actually complete the task. Therefore, your capability to perform the necessary task will be effortless. There will be times when you seek external help to counter your areas of weakness, but it is up to you to recognize and resist any and all distractions to you fulfilling the *Call*.

BEFORE YOU QUIT YOUR JOB

OK, we are almost at the launch discussion, but before we go there, I would like to briefly talk to those of you who may be considering quitting your job. I know you are probably both scared and excited right now about your *Calling*. However, I want to reiterate what I said before, don't up and quit your job to pursue your *Purpose* without a plan. It is crucial that you take the time to develop a well-thought plan of action before giving your 2-weeks' notice.

For those of you looking to change jobs or positions, start your search while you are still working. If possible, start the search within the company you are working for. Inquire about your desired position inside the company.

Maybe there isn't a current position that aligns with your *Zone of Greatness*, but there's a possibility one can be created. This requires that you schedule an appointment with your direct supervisor, manager, HR to discuss what you are interested in doing. Do your research beforehand and come prepared to show them the benefits of creating a new position. You never know what opportunities may be available for you.

If finding an alignment at your current employer isn't possible, or you're not currently employed, go ahead and start implementing your marketing strategy. Once you've secured the new job or position, then submit your 2-weeks' notice.

For those who are looking to start a business, please learn from my mistakes. When I discovered the next phase of what I wanted to do, I quit my job too soon and suffered as a result. So, before you quit, here is what I suggest:

- Take stock of your monthly expenses and income. Physically, sit down and write or type it out.

189

- Determine if any of the expenses cited can be eliminated. If so, eliminate them and start putting the monthly amount you were paying in savings, cd, or a money market account.

- Before quitting your job, ensure that you have at least 2–3 years' worth of monthly expenses available in your savings.

– OR –

- Become what's called a *Parallel-Preneur*, someone who works a job and also has a business. You can start your venture part-time or full-time while you are still working your job.

- Your job will cover your monthly expenses and help with some of the expenses needed for your venture.

- Once you are able to generate at least 1.5–2 times the income you make on your job via your business – then consider quitting your job.

- I still recommend that you have at the least a 12-month emergency fund in savings first.

I'm of the belief that whatever it is you are *Called* to do, will generate revenue directly or indirectly; however, it will take some time to build it. Trust me, you don't want to struggle financially while you build it, especially if you have others depending on you to take care of them.

On the flipside, if your faith muscle has been built, and you can boldly step out and launch full-time – ignore everything I just said and do it!!!

CHAPTER THIRTEEN:

GREAT. LET THE WORLD SEE IT!

Vision without action is a dream. Action without vision is simply passing the time. Action with Vision is making a positive difference.[124] *– Joel Barker*

Well OK, at this point, you have everything you need to launch your vision into motion.

If you are anything like me, you're probably feeling pressure and let's keep it real, this is a ~~little~~ lot frightening. It's very real at this point and the voices in your head are louder than ever before. You've probably already come up with a number of reasons why **now** is **not** the time to move forward on this.

With that in mind, I want you to take a moment and write down every obstacle and reason why this is not the right time, that you can come up with. Get it all out, every single barrier that is currently standing in your way of achieving your *Purpose* today...use the template in the *Destiny Starter™ Workbook, Activity 11* or grab some paper and a notebook, put the book down, and start writing.

Now, for every obstacle, reason, or barrier that you identified, I want you to rewrite them from the perspective of possibility using the word **but** and an option that counters what you wrote. *For example, between work and my family commitments, I just don't have the time to do this right now...but, I can get up 30-minutes earlier and use a portion of my lunch period each day to work on this.*

So, go ahead and put the book down again and get to writing. Let me just reiterate here, you were made for this and don't let anyone tell you differently or allow anything to stop you. Even you!

Now that we've gotten that out of the way...**what's the launch date again?**

If you didn't designate a launch date previously, I want you to schedule it right now. Pull out your calendar and add it. Then tell your family and friends about what you are doing and the actual date of your official launch.

While speaking with them, get some ideas of what you can do to celebrate the launch. It doesn't have to be anything super large, unless you want it to be, but make it memorable.

GET YOUR NETWORKING ON

Back in *Chapter 10*, we talked about identifying your network, those you are already connected to and those you want to connect with. Here is where you put that work to action.

Active networking occurs through making and nurturing connections with people by attending events, utilizing social media, volunteering, and helping others. I have heard many people say, *the easiest or quickest way to get what you want is by helping others get what they want.*

So that could look like reaching out to someone on your *Tier 3: Audience* list, letting them know you would like to learn from them, and asking if there is anything you can do to help them do what they do, while you learn in the process. The key here is – when you know where you want to go, it is essential that you start networking and talking about it with others.

It has been said, where it once was six degrees of separation, with the emergence and growth of social media, we are now at about 2–3 degrees of separation. That's 2–3 people away from those you need to connect with to advance your career or business. With that, everyone on your list in *Tier 1: Allies* and *Tier 2: Associates* should know where you are looking to go and what you want to do. You never know who is connected to who; remember there's only 2-3 degrees of separation. So that means, I am 2-3 people away to being connected to Oprah Winfrey and Tony Robbins. I'm just saying!

DON'T LEAVE MOMENTUM TO CHANCE

I once heard a podcast message from thought leader and radio host, Dave Ramsey, talking about momentum. He said, *"People tend to think momentum just occurs randomly, but it's not how it happens. It doesn't happen by accident, it's a process that gets you there."*[125] This process he called the *Momentum Theorem*:

THE MOMENTUM THEOREM

$$\frac{Fi}{T}(G)=M$$

Focused Intensity, Over Time, Multiplied by God (Infinite), Equals Unstoppable Momentum

The **"F"** in the formula is *focused*. Gary Keller, author of the *One Thing*, said, *"Extraordinary results are directly determined by how narrow you can make your focus. You need to be doing fewer things for more effect instead of doing more things with side effects."*[126] When you step into the *Call*, I know there's so much that you can do, and you can do all of those things; just not all at once. Pick one thing, and one thing only to focus on. Then as you succeed and advance, start adding if you choose.

Next is the "i" for *intensity*. When we are talking about the *Call* – intensity is a given because you are doing something you are passionate about. Every time, and I mean, every time I think or talk about my *Call*, I get excited. It's an unconscious occurrence that happens, and when I start working on it, that passion intensifies. Keller said, *"Passion for something leads to disproportionate time practicing or working at it. That time spent eventually translates to skill, and when skill improves, results improve. Better results generally lead to more enjoyment, and more passion and more time invested. It can be a virtuous cycle all the way to extraordinary results."*[126]

Then we have the "T" which stands for *time*. Momentum is not an overnight success story. It happens as a result of focused intensity over time. That's consistently doing what you do in excellence, over and over again and again, and again. Ramsey said, *"If you can be [focused and] intense for over a decade, you will become a national brand."*[125]

And the last letter of the formula is "G" for *God (higher power, universe – whatever you believe)*. When we multiply focused intensity over time by God, you don't just get momentum, but you get Unstoppable Momentum. Ramsey said, *"Anything multiplied by infinite equals infinite on the other end."*[125]

Focused Intensity, Over Time, Multiplied by God (Infinite), Equals Unstoppable Momentum!

DON'T LET FEAR STOP YOU

In preparation for this book, I did a *Facebook* poll. The question I asked was *why do you believe most people in our world today never fulfill their Destiny while on earth?* Or to state it another way, *what barriers can*

you think of that prevent or hinder people from walking in their Purpose?
Below are the responses I received:

> *"Lack of faith or belief. Many people look at their current situations and look at their goal and don't feel that they can get to that goal due to their current situation. With faith in God all things are possible, and we should apply faith in all that we do. We all have the power to be successful, we just need to believe it."*
> – Angel Johnson, Former President of *National Association of Black Accountants (NABA)* – Milwaukee

> *"Feeling like it's never the right time to get started."*
> – Briana Melissa Ford, Founder of *Startup Noire*

> *"These are all such great answers. The only other thing that I would add here is the willingness to make the sacrifices that are necessary to see your Purpose come to fruition. We live in such an instantaneous society, that often, when we don't see the result immediately, we choose another path. Purpose, I believe, is a lifelong journey. There will be learning curves, disappointments, but there will also be victories in the midst of the growing pains. I think at times when we don't get that instant gratification of success, we get discouraged and don't see it come to fruition."*
> – Cecelia Marlow, Vice President, *Federal Savings Bank*

> *"Distraction can be a barrier or hinder one from their God-given Purpose. Oftentimes we can have what it takes, do the appropriate things, but be going in the wrong direction. At this point, the vision/Purpose is delayed. One goal would be to learn to hear from God and be clear on your Purpose."*
> – Chareda Shelton-Carter, Managing Broker, *UHEB Inc.*

> *"The first step is realizing your Purpose. We get in the general area, but as it relates to fine tuning and understanding the end result, that requires spiritual guidance and vision. It's like buying a house. You find the neighborhood and maybe even the house, but it's when the Realtor opens the door and you walk around in it – you figure out it's YOUR home. People find houses but not always a home."*
> – Denisha Tate, Founder, *Denisha Tate & Associates, LLC*

> *"Fear of failure and lack of faith! Sometimes our God-given Purpose does not feel as comfortable as the area we are used to operating in and it takes a bit of risk-taking and operation of one's faith to step out of this comfort zone."*
> – DeVona Wright Cottrell, Associate General Counsel, *R.W. Baird*

> *"Our biggest hindrance is ourselves. Oftentimes it's because we 'failed before' and we are therefore afraid to try again. Reality for me is I don't believe in failure. I don't believe in not being prepared, which results in an unsuccessful outcome or one we didn't expect. Motto: when preparation meets opportunity = success. It may not be on the scale you anticipated, but the success of completion is always rewarding. Yassss!"*

– Kimberly R. Lock, Founder, *KRL Publishing*

"Focusing on what others have and not recognizing the gifts God gave you to use."
– La'Ketta Denise Caldwell, Founder, *KetaLife*

"A big factor is Fear – we all experience this. Another factor is lack of confidence, feeling incapable of achieving a goal or unworthy."
– Renee Dabney, Author, Owner, *The Write Bud*

BE AFRAID AND DO IT ANYWAY

The results of the *Facebook* poll revealed that **fear**, and the remnants thereof, is the common denominator for most of the responses. Fear has a major impact on our lives. In its most basic form, fear is an important response to danger. It connects us to our fight, flight, or freeze response – the body's natural way of reacting to perceived dangers or threats.

On the flipside, fear can also foster adrenaline, action, and intrigue. If directed appropriately, fear can make way for courage, possibility, persistence, and motivation. I'm not suggesting that you not have or even suppress fear, but that you embrace your fears. Be afraid and still step out and walk in your *Calling* to do the impossible, to walk boldly in your *Greatness*. Let fear be the catalyst that activates your *Greatness* as opposed to the element that stifles your progress and growth.

Best-selling author and virtual mentor, Michael Hyatt, once said, *"When I begin to feel anxious, I tell myself, my body is just preparing itself for peak performance."*[127] He has completely changed his perspective of fear and anxiety, and fully embraces it.

Therefore, as you move forward, I challenge you to embrace fear as it arises and shift the way you think about it. As opposed to allowing fear to stifle your progress, think on the words on the next page. Come back to it as a reminder of where to focus whenever fear surfaces.

Preparation Direction Sacrificial Faith Clarity Prayer Belief Confidence Taking Patience Worthy Risk Goals Proactivity Inspiration Possibility Initiative Motivation Productivity Guidance Courage Spiritual Vision Focus Persistence Training

THE POWER OF DEFINING MOMENTS

As we close out this phase of the book, I want to briefly talk about this concept that has been weighing heavily on my mind. I call it *"The Power of Defining Moments."*

There's something to be said about being prepared when opportunity comes. In those moments when preparation and opportunity meet, magical things happen.

Let me give you an example. I was strolling through my Facebook feed and came across an *American Idol* video clip. In the clip was a young lady named Courtney Timmons[128] who had dreamed of becoming a singer. She heard about the *American Idol* auditions at the last minute, and arrived onsite to register. Unfortunately, she had missed the deadline to participate, and was told that registration is closed.

As you can imagine, the young lady was distraught. Although disappointed, she decided to stay outside the arena. She was noticed by many who were coming and going, and later in the day, Ryan

197

Seacrest, the host of the show, approached her. He inquired why she was out there looking sad, and the young lady shared her story.

His heart was touched, and he asked her to follow him up to the judging room. He told her that he couldn't make any promises as to whether the judges would see her or not, but he would get her to the room.

They walked into the judging room with Lionel Richie, Katy Perry, and Luke Bryan, who allowed her to audition on the spot. When this young lady opened her mouth to sing, you should've seen the expressions on the faces of the judges, and everyone else in the room. Her voice was absolutely beautiful. She had her own style and flavor that completely controlled the room.

Her singing brought Ryan Seacrest and Katy Perry to tears. Needless to say, the young lady was given a *Golden Ticket* to *Hollywood*. For her, that was a defining moment. Although she wasn't supposed to be there, an opportunity presented itself, she was prepared, and then the magic happened.

Just as it did with Courtney Timmons, opportunity will come knocking. My question for you is, *will you be prepared for your defining moment?*

✎ DESTINY STARTER™ WORKBOOK

See Activity Twelve (12) in the *Destiny Starter™ Workbook* to compose your barriers and buts.

BRINGING IT ALL TOGETHER

As we conclude *Marker Three – Execution: Do It* of the *Destiny Starter™ RoadMap*, let's review...

In this section, we added the finishing touches to the amazingly great vision that you have to impact our world. We've talked about faith – the cornerstone to your success – eliminating impossibilities, scheduling your official launch, sharing your vision with others, and the recipe for building momentum. In addition, we talked about working through fear and being prepared for the opportunities that are coming your way. Essentially, you have everything that you need to do this, and to do this well.

I want to encourage you to not let anything deprive you or strip your *Destiny* away from you. Remember, walking boldly in your *Greatness* is the way to happiness and fulfillment in life.

So, as we have done at the end of each section – it is time to celebrate the completion of *Marker Three – Execution.*

WooHoo – I'm sincerely so excited for you. Now come on, **You Got This!!!**

From My Heart to Yours

THE COST OF SAYING YES TO THE CALL

Let me share with you a little well-kept secret: there is a *Cost* to saying **Yes** to the *Call!!!* On your *Destiny Path*, there will be some things that you must sacrifice along the way, and there is no way around it.

One day, I watched a video on *YouTube*[129] with Steven Furtick and Bishop T.D. Jakes. In the video, T.D. Jakes was sharing the **Cost of the Call** on his life. He started talking about a Bishop he ran into in the airport who told him, *"You've lost something you will never get back – you've lost normalcy."*

Jakes said, *"I was distracted by the explosion, but I will come to see the damage...I will see in the tears of my children, the pregnancy of my daughter, the pains of my son...holding my wife in tears. I would hold her in tears and preach faith, then go home and lay down in a bed of fear. I would say, 'God, where have you taken me!' I almost quit! ...I never even asked to be big, I wanted to be effective, not famous...famous is the consequence of being effective. When I saw how much it cost, I told God, 'You can have this back.'"*

Later in the conversation, Jakes went on to say, the moment he began to tell God, *"Thank you, but no thank you sir, you can have this back"*...a lady crossed his path. She said, *"Bishop Jakes I've been in the hospital, I was pregnant in my fallopian tubes, and the baby died there. I was carrying around a dead baby and the toxicity from the baby almost killed me. The only thing that kept me alive was hearing you preach. If you hadn't been preaching to me every day, I would've died."* Then she looked at him and said, *"It's for us, it's not for them (those that ridicule you, that lie on you, that talk about you behind your back, etc.); it's for us."*

Bishop Jakes said, *"It hit me so hard, I got in my car and cried all the way back to my room – because she reminded me Why I was there!"* She reminded him of the *Why* behind the *Call* on his life!

He said, *"If it were not for that woman,"* he would've quit...

Then he said, *"When you talk about what it Costs, simply everything!!!"*

Because of this, it is crucial that you pinpoint your *Why* in the very beginning. It's the *Why* that keeps you inspired, that keeps you motivated, that's keeps you going, despite anything that happens.

The *Why* keeps you connected to the *Call* and, most importantly, to the *Creator!*

– Anita "AC" Clinton

Marker Four

Accountability: Grow It

OVERVIEW

GROW IT

Motivation gets you going, and habit gets you there.[130] – Zig Ziglar

W ell here we are, at the last marker of the *Destiny Starter™ RoadMap* called *Accountability: Grow It!* In this final section, we will talk about the importance of networking and connecting with like-minded individuals who are able to support and hold you accountable to growing your venture.

In addition, we discuss the importance of ongoing training and development. You can never have too much information unless you are just gathering and not applying. As you progress inside your vision, it is vital that you continue to be stretched along the way.

Lastly, we will wrap it all up with useful tools and resources that are available to you. So, let's get to it!

CHAPTER FOURTEEN:

IRON SHARPENS IRON

As iron sharpens iron, so one person sharpens another.[131] *– Proverbs 27:17*

So, you've discovered your *Purpose* or the *Call* on your life, composed your plan and are preparing to or have already launched. You may be thinking, *Now What?* Do I have to do this alone?

Nope, you don't have to go it alone.

There is a concept called mastermind groups, introduced by 20th Century thought leader, Napoleon Hill. He defined them as *"a friendly alliance with one or more persons who will encourage one to follow through with both plan and purpose...Every mind needs friendly contact with other minds, for food of expansion and growth."*[132]

Because I know firsthand that it can be extremely lonely on this *Destiny Path*, we have developed what we call *Be Great ThinkPods*. The *ThinkPods* are mastermind groups that are uniquely designed to bring together like-minded individuals who are serious about walking boldly in their *Purpose*. The members of the group will provide support and accountability, share ideas, and leverage each other's collective experience in the spirit of love, honesty, and respect.

Here is what you need to know about the *ThinkPods*:

ThinkPods Goals and Objectives

- Gain new insights and explore new possibilities – tune into untapped potential and resources.

- Focus in on short-term goals – specifically action items that support the vision.

- See real, measurable progress in respective ventures.

- Develop an immediate and reliable support network. Think of it as a personal advisory board.

- Tap into inspiration and positive energy to carry you into the days and weeks that follow.

It's great to have people you can bounce ideas off of, to share tools, resources, techniques that can help you along the way. Whether you choose to join our group, join another group, or create your own – I want to encourage you to get connected with a group or someone to hold you accountable and ensure that you stay on the right path.

For more information or to apply for the *ThinkPod* groups, visit www.begreatglobal.com/thinkpods.

Other Options

If groups are not your thing, consider investing in a coach or consultant if you can afford it. Like everything else, you want to do your due diligence before hiring a coach/consultant.

Start with specifically defining what you want from a coach or consultant, and what your expectations are for the time you spend with him or her. For example, are you looking for accountability, or are you looking to break through something in your life or business, etc.? Get clear on what you want, then start your research.

You want to know their area of expertise or focus, and you want to review testimonials from past clients. Most coaches will offer an initial consultation call. This is your opportunity to get your questions/concerns addressed, and for both of you to determine if this would be a good fit. You want to keep searching until you pinpoint the best coach to meet your needs.

For information about my consulting services, visit www.anitaclinton.com/consulting.

CHAPTER FIFTEEN:

TOOLS AND RESOURCES

Tell me and I forget, teach me and I may remember, involve me and I learn.[133]
– Benjamin Franklin

I believe that with information, knowledge, and understanding, coupled with action – there isn't much one can't do. In fact, we live in this age of unlimited information. You can go to *Google* and *YouTube* to find out how to do just about anything.

At *Be Great Global*, we understand that the plethora of internet resources can be overwhelming. Therefore, we are committed to providing you with access to a variety of resources:

- Original content designed with you in mind.

- Curated content from experts, thought leaders, and others.

- Free and premium products, tutorials, and training programs.

- Recommended professionals for brand development, printing, creative design, etc.

- Marketing tools and other tips and tricks.

Content is being added on a consistent basis, so be sure to check periodically at www.begreatglobal.com. In addition, join the *BG Squad* and stay up-to-date on all new material and resources as they become available.

✎ DESTINY STARTER™ WORKBOOK

You will find a full list of resources in the *Destiny Starter™ Workbook*.

BRINGING IT ALL TOGETHER

A s we conclude *Marker Four – Accountability: Grow It* of the *Destiny Starter™ RoadMap*, let's just take a moment to exhale...I totally get that this is a lot to consume. But I want to recite something to you:

You were created to be extraordinary. Your life should matter, your time on earth should be impactful. People should know you were here because of the impact your Calling had on making our world a better place.

And the last thing that I want to leave you with is, **You Got This!** And we will be here to help wherever possible. So, don't hesitate to reach out to us at www.destinystarterbook.com/share.

I promise to do my best to respond personally or on the *Be Great Global Podcast.*

AFTERWORD

It's been a long time coming. Thank God for this day.[134] *– Alan Crotzer*

This book has been in the works in some form or fashion since 2009. I originally finished the first draft of this book in 2010, sent it out to 10 friends for review and put it on my bookshelf. It resided there for 8 years. I would pick it up off and on over the years, but the time wasn't right yet.

I know so much more now than I did back then. I had to learn so many valuable lessons in order to complete and share this book with the world.

Words can't express the gratitude and the joy that I feel at this point in time. The finished product is everything and more than I even imagined it could be...praise be to God.

My prayer is that the book has blessed you, and has motivated and empowered you to discover, strategize, and execute the *Call* on your life. And *Be Great Global* is here to help you at every step along the way.

Our vision is 1 billion morally conscious, ethical dreamers walking boldly in their *Greatness* and transforming the face of our world.

Now this vision is huge, and we can't possibly do it alone. We need your help. If you've gotten anything from reading this book, visiting our website, listening to our podcast, please share the information with your family and friends. The more people we can get connected to their dreams, the better our world becomes.

We look forward to seeing you show up in the world.

Step-by-Step Through Launching Your Dream
DESTINY
STARTER
BOOK
MASTERCLASS & DIGITAL COURSE
www.destinystarterbook.com

BE GREAT
Global
MAKE A LIVING DOING WORK YOU ACTUALLY
LOVE
Check Out The
Be Great
Global Podcast
Listen on
Apple Podcasts
Listen on
STITCHER
Listen on
Spotify
BE GREAT
Global Podcast
HAPPINESS.
FULFILLMENT.
MONEY.
www.begreatglobal.com

ABOUT ANITA "AC" CLINTON

With almost two decades of creative design, brand development, marketing, editorial, and business development experience, Anita "AC" Clinton is the go-to-person for all aspects of purpose. Her passion resides in helping *Dreamers* connect to their purpose, and transition to *Game-Changers*. Despite setbacks, roadblocks and wrong turns along the way, she is living proof that anything can be accomplished with tenacity, determination, and perseverance.

Of the many challenges impacting our world today, I am convinced that the answers rest inside each of us. We are the problem-solvers, created for this moment in time, and the world is waiting on the manifestation of our Greatness. Not only are we well-equipped to solve the world's problems – but true happiness and fulfillment in life are found when we connect with the Call on our lives. To put it clearly, we will Love what we do! How Awesome is that?

Anita is the Founder and President of *Anita Clinton Enterprises, LLC,* (ACE), and *Be Great Global* (BGG), where she creates the *Be Great Global Podcast,* books, and training programs to help intrapreneurs and entrepreneurs find happiness, fulfillment, and money doing work they actually love. Inside her efforts, she envisions a world where the masses are walking boldly in their *Greatness* and transforming the face of our world.

Over the years, Anita has used her experience and wealth of knowledge to help solopreneurs, entrepreneurs, small businesses, and non-profits execute their vision.

Connect with Anita "AC" Clinton on *Facebook, Twitter, Instagram, LinkedIn* and *Pinterest* **@acclinton1.**

NOTES

From My Heart to Yours
[1] James Dean quote from the Brainy Quote website, https://www.brainyquote.com/quotes/james_dean_103528.

Introduction
[2] Marianne Williamson quote from the Brainy Quote website, https://www.brainyquote.com/quotes/marianne_williamson_400880.
[3] Myles Munroe website, https://www.mylesmunroeinternational.com.
[4] Dictionary.com website, https://www.dictionary.com/browse/greatness.
[5] The Rare Recordings of Napoleon Hill One, YouTube video, Mike Pino, October 2, 2013, https://youtu.be/N3hERcahJ9g.
[6] Oprah on Taking Responsibility for Your Life | Oprah's Lifeclass | Oprah Winfrey Network, YouTube video, OWN, https://youtu.be/Dp_cmLfJZ1wOprah.

From My Heart to Yours
[7] Dr. Seuss quote from the Rare website, https://rare.us/rare-life/quotes-rare-life/be-who-you-are/.

Overview: Find It
[8] Jim Rohn quote from QuoteFancy website, https://quotefancy.com/quote/23202/Jim-Rohn-If-you-really-want-to-do-something-you-ll-find-a-way-If-you-don-t-you-ll-find-an.
[9] Brad Lomenick, H3 Leadership (HarperCollins Leadership, 2015).

Chapter One: What's Your Passion?
[10] T.D. Jakes quote from QuoteFancy website, https://quotefancy.com/quote/945646/T-D-Jakes-If-you-can-t-figure-out-your-purpose-figure-out-your-passion-For-your-passion.
[11] Oprah Winfrey quote from BrainyQuote website, https://www.brainyquote.com/quotes/oprah_winfrey_384837.
[12] Napoleon Hill, Think and Grow Rich (TarcherPerigee; Revised & Enlarged Edition, August 2005).
[13] Forrest Whitaker Winning Best Actor, YouTube Video, Oscar, April 24, 2008, https://youtu.be/4-fGCHGTaGE.
[14] Wall Street Journal website, www.wsj.com/articles/forest-whitakers-character-studies-1481296906.
[15] Dr. Martin Luther King Jr quote from Goodreads.com, https://www.goodreads.com/quotes/317902-we-are-prone-to-judge-success-by-the-index-of.

Chapter Two: Pinpoint Your Genius
[16] Denis Diderot quote from BrainyQuote website, https://www.brainyquote.com/quotes/denis_diderot_403220.
[17] Oxford Dictionary website, www.oxforddictionaries.com, www.lexico.com.
[18] Thomas Edison quote from Notable Quotes website, www.notable-quotes.com/g/genius_quotes.html#gMqwg1425zhHXfv7.99.

[19] Reisinger, Don, Here's How Many iPhones Are Currently Being Used Worldwide, blog, www.fortune.com/2017/03/06/apple-iphone-use-worldwide.

Chapter Three: The Gift of Service

[20] Dr. Albert Schweitzer quote from BrainyQuote website, www.brainyquote.com/quotes/authors/a/albert_schweitzer.html.

[21] Lim W. M., Understanding the selfie phenomenon: current insights and future research directions, Emerald Insight, September 12, 2016, https://www.emeraldinsight.com/doi/abs/10.1108/EJM-07-2015-0484.

[22] Bill Gate's story, www.biography.com.

[23] George Washington Carver quote from BrainyQuote website, www.brainyquote.com/quotes/authors/g/george_washington_carver.html#QlWhHLgB 69K0rifI.99,
Charlene Aaron, "George Washington Carver: Master Inventor, Artist," blog, www.cbn.com/cbnnews/us/2010/February/George-Washington-Carver-Master-Inventor-Artist.

[24] Henry Ford from Biography website, www.biography.com/business-figure/henry-ford.

[25] Martin Luther King Jr. from Biography website, www.biography.com/activist/martin-luther-king-jr.

[26] Mother Teresa from Biography website, www.biography.com/religious-figure/mother-teresa.

[27] Oprah Winfrey website, www.oprah.com.

From My Heart to Yours

[28] Bishop T.D. Jakes Beware of 3 Types of Friends, YouTube, T.D. Jakes TV, March 24, 2014, https://youtu.be/bc8o4KuThBE.

Overview: Plan It

[29] Dave Ramsey, https://www.daveramsey.com/.

From My Heart to Yours

[30] Merriam-Webster website, https://www.merriam-webster.com/dictionary/possibility.

[31] Confucius quote from QuoteFancy website, https://quotefancy.com/quote/66103/Confucius-The-man-who-thinks-he-can-and-the-man-who-thinks-he-can-t-are-both-right.

[32] Nelson Mandela from The Nobel Prize website, www.nobelprize.org/prizes/peace/1993/ceremony-speech.

Chapter Four: Life's Training Obstacles

[33] Lucinda Moore, Growing Up Maya Angelou, blog, www.smithsonianmag.com/arts-culture/growing-up-maya-angelou-79582387/?no-ist.

[34] Dr. Maya Angelou website, www.mayaangelou.com/biography.

[35] Dr. Maya Angelou, Still I Rise, Poetry Foundation, https://www.poetryfoundation.org/poems/46446/still-i-rise.

[36] Joyce Meyer, Abuse and the Miracle of Recovery, blog, www.joycemeyer.org/everydayanswers/ea-teachings/abuse-and-the-miracle-of-recovery.

[37] Joyce Meyer, The Poison of Unforgiveness, blog, www.joycemeyer.org/everydayanswers/ea-teachings/the-poison-of-unforgiveness.

[38] William P. Young, The Shack, (Windblown Media; 1st edition 2007).

[39] Vocabulary.com website, https://www.vocabulary.com/dictionary/vulnerability.

[40] Brene Brown from Ted website, The Power of Vulnerability, www.ted.com/talks/brene_brown_on_vulnerability?language=en.

Chapter Five: Renewing You

[41] Goodreads.com website, https://www.goodreads.com/quotes/8683366-self-care-is-a-deliberate-choice-to-gift-ourself-with-people.

[42] Dionne Van Zyl, The Power of the Human Spirit, blog, https://wiredliving.org/blog/the-power-of-the-human-spirit, (2017).

[43] Dictionary.com website, https://www.dictionary.com/browse/attitude. BusinessDictionary website, www.businessdictionary.com/definition/attitude.html.

[44] Zig Ziglar, Secrets of Closing the Sale, (Revell, a division of Baker Publishing Group, 2003).

[45] Viktor Frankl, Man's Search for Meaning, (Verlag für Jugend und Volk – Austria, 1946) (Beacon Press – U.S., 1959).

[46] Les Brown quote from QuoteFancy, https://quotefancy.com/quote/853150/Les-Brown-Change-your-thinking-Change-your-life-Your-thoughts-create-your-reality.

[47] Dr. IV Hilliard, Mental Toughness for Success, (Light Publications, 2003).

[48] As A Man Thinketh: An Inspirational Classic Comes to Life (based on the book by James Allen), Directed by Jon Miller, Miller Media and Pitcher Point Productions, 2017. Amazon Prime Video, https://www.Amazon.com/As-Man-Thinketh-Thought-classic/dp/B078Z318SC.

[49] King James Version, Bible Gateway, 1993, https://www.biblegateway.com/passage/?search=proverbs+18%3A21&version=KJV.

[50] Detoxing Your Mind: An Interview with Dr. Caroline Leaf, YouTube, Elevation Church, September 8, 2019, https://youtu.be/Ea8pHeetkgo.

[51] Saul McLeod, Cognitive Dissonance, Simply Psychology website, www.simplypsychology.org/cognitive-dissonance.html.

[52] Bill Winston, The Law of Confession, (Harris House Inc, 2012).

[53] Hill, Napoleon, Three Feet From Gold, (Sterling Publishing, 2009).

[54] Judge Lynn Toler, Divorce Court, www.divorce.com.

[55] John Wiley & Sons, Inc., The DISc Profile, https://www.discprofile.com, 1928-2017.

[56] NERIS Analytics Limited, 16 Personalities, https://www.16personalities.com.

[57] Katherine Cook Briggs and Isabel Briggs Myers, Myers-Briggs Type Indicator, https://www.myersbriggs.org/.

[58] Don Clifton, Clifton StrengthsFinder Assessment, www.strengthsfinder.com.

[59] Dmitry Golubnichy, High5 Test, https://high5test.com.

[60] The Enneagram Institute, Riso-Hudson Enneagram Type Indicator, https://www.enneagraminstitute.com/.

[61] VIA Institute of Character, The VIA Character Strengths Survey, www.viacharacter.org.

[62] Gretchen Rubin, The Four Tendencies, (Harmony, 2017).

Chapter Six: What's the Vision?

[63] Steve Jobs quote from Move Me Quotes & More website, https://www.movemequotes.com/top-10-steve-jobs-quotes/.

[64] Merriam-Webster website, https://www.merriam-webster.com/dictionary/vision.

[65] Lexico by Oxford website, www.lexico.com/en/definition/vision.

[66] Bishop Tudor Bismark, The Golden Age, YouTube, True Word Of Yeshua, February 11, 2014, https://youtu.be/lf4wtv9ZaJU.

67 7 Mountains of Culture, http://www.ywamkosova.com/the-7-mountains-of-influence/.
68 Lance Wallnau Explains The Seven Mountains Mandate, YouTube Video, Bruce Wilson, July 16, 2009, https://youtu.be/qQbGnJd9poc, www.lancewallnau.com/.
69 Barry Scheck and Peter Neufel, Innocence Project, https://www.innocenceproject.org, 1992.
70 Will Kenton, Intrapreneurship, blog, https://www.investopedia.com/terms/i/intrapreneurship.asp (2020).
71 Statista Research Department, Unit sales of Sony's PlayStation consoles worldwide from 2011 to 2019 (in millions), by quarter, https://www.statista.com/statistics/222403/unit-sales-of-sonys-gaming-hardware-by-category/, February 19, 2020.
72 Merriam-Webster website, www.merriam-webster.com/dictionary/avatar.
73 Hubspot, Customer Avatar Workbook, www.cdn2.hubspot.net/hub/18316/file-13370555-pdf/.../customer-avatar-workbook.pdf.
74 Seth Godin, Tribes, (Penguin Group, 2008).
75 United States Patent and Trademark Office website, www.uspto.gov.
76 United States Copyright Office website, www.copyright.gov.

Chapter Seven: Start Writing the Plan
77 Robert H. Schuller, You Can Become the Person You Want To Be, Page 24, (Hawthorn Books, New York, 1973).
78 Dictionary.com website, https://www.dictionary.com/browse/mentor.
79 Gail Matthews, PhD, Research Study, Dominican University of California, http://www.goalband.co.uk/the-research.html.
80 Americans for Community Development, What is the L3C?, www.americansforcommunitydevelopment.org/.

Chapter Eight: Your Brand Matters
81 Alina Wheeler, Designing Identity, (John Wiley & Sons, Inc., 2013).
82 Investopedia website, https://www.investopedia.com/terms/b/brand.asp.
83 Gretchen N. Foley, MD and Julie P. Gentile, MD, Nonverbal Communication in Psychotherapy, National Center for Biotechnology Information, U.S. National Library of Medicine, blog, https://www.ncbi.nlm.nih.gov/pmc/articles/PMC2898840/#B1.
84 Léandre Larouche, How to End a Cover Letter with a Call to Action, blog, https://www.jobscan.co/blog/how-to-end-a-cover-letter (2020).
85 Roger Constandse, Writing a Compelling Vision Statement, blog, www.timethoughts.com/goalsetting/vision-statements.htm.
86 The Walt Disney Company website, www.thewaltdisneycompany.com.
87 Be Great Global website, www.begreatglobal.com.
Susan G. Komen website, https://ww5.komen.org/AboutUs/OurWork.html.
Cradles to Crayons website, https://www.cradlestocrayons.org/what-we-do/our-mission-and-model/.
88 Disneyland website, https://disneyland.disney.go.com/.
89 Hubspot, 27 Companies with Really Catchy Slogans & Brand Taglines, blog, https://blog.hubspot.com/marketing/brand-slogans-and-taglines.
Alina Wheeler, Designing Identity, (John Wiley & Sons, Inc., 2013).
90 Jackie Fenn and Mark Raskino, Mastering the Hype Cycle: How to Choose the Right Innovation at the Right Time, (Harvard Business Press, 2008).
91 Stripe website, www.stripe.com.
Evernote website, www.evernote.com.

Fundly website, www.fundly.com.

Hubspot website, www.hubspot.com.

[92] Neil Patel, What a Unique Selling Proposition Really Means & Why Your Business Must Have One, blog, www.neilpatel.com/blog/unique-selling-proposition.

[93] Wikipedia website, www.wikipedia.org/wiki/Hex.

[94] Dan Miller, Building a Storybrand, (HarperCollins Publishers, 2017).

[95] An Era of Growth: The Cross-Platform Report Q4 2013, https://www.nielsen.com/us/en/insights/report/2014/an-era-of-growth-the-cross-platform-report/, The Nielson Company.

[96] Ian Blair, 4 Ways Your Business Can Benefit From Having a Mobile App, blog, https://buildfire.com/ways-business-benefit-having-mobile-app/.

[97] Investopedia website, www.investopedia.com/terms/m/media-kit.asp.

Chapter Nine: Simplify Your Marketing

[98] Peter Drucker quote from BrainyQuote website, www.brainyquote.com/quotes/peter_drucker_154444.

[99] Amanda Augustine, CPCC & CPRW, The Importance of Networking (and How to Do It Well), blog, https://www.topresume.com/career-advice/importance-of-networking-for-career-success.

[100] Bob Burg quote from More Famous Quotes website, http://www.morefamousquotes.com/topics/quotes-about-cultivating-relationships/.

[101] Faith Popcorn, www.faithpopcorn.com/.

[102] The National Bureau of Economic Research, www.nber.org/.

[103] Ken Blanchard, Phil Hodges, and Phyllis Hendry, Lead Like Jesus – Revisited, (W Publishing Group, an Imprint of Thomas Nelson, 2016).

[104] Freelancers Union and Upwork, Freelancing in America: 2017, (Conducted by Edelman Intelligence), https://s3.Amazonaws.com/fuwt-prod-storage/content/FreelancingInAmericaReport-2017.pdf.

Wikipedia website, https://en.wikipedia.org/wiki/Freelancer.

[105] Will Kenton, Virtual Assistant, Investopedia, blog, https://www.investopedia.com/terms/v/virtual-assistant.asp (2020).

[106] Chris Smith, BGR, Making the $1,249 iPhone XS only costs Apple $443, www.nypost.com/2018/09/26/making-the-1249-iphone-xs-only-costs-apple-443/.

[107] InfusionSoft/Keap, Sales Funnel Management, blog, www.keap.com/product/sales-funnel.

[108] Alexa, What is a Key Performance Indicator (KPI), https://blog.alexa.com/marketing-research/kpi/.

Chapter Ten: Finish Writing the Plan

[109] Earl Nightingale quote from *BrainyQuote* website, https://www.brainyquote.com/quotes/earl_nightingale_159044.

[110] Business Model Canvas website, www.businessmodelgeneration.com.

Overview: Do It

[111] Robert Griffin, III, quote from Quotefancy website, https://quotefancy.com/quote/1219795/Robert-Griffin-III-Hard-work-pays-off-hard-work-beats-talent-any-day-but-if-you-re.

Chapter Eleven: Can You See It?

[112] Zig Ziglar, You Were Born to Win, https://www.ziglar.com/quotes/you-were-born-to-win-but-to-be-a-winner/.

[113] John C. Maxwell, Our Road Map For Success: You Can Get There from Here, (HarperCollins Leadership, 2002).

Chapter Twelve: Faith to Do the Impossible

[114] Saint Augustine quote from BrainyQuote website, https://www.brainyquote.com/quotes/saint_augustine_121380?src=t_faith.

[115] The Cliff Young Story by Jack Canfield, YouTube video, Videos4Motivation, June 29, 2012, https://youtu.be/5WXXm-FVB58.

[116] Chris Gardner website, www.chrisgardnermedia.com.

[117] Wikipedia website, https://en.wikipedia.org/wiki/Susan_Boyle.

[118] Wikipedia website, https://en.wikipedia.org/wiki/Michael_Jordan.

[119] Mary Kay website, www.marykay.com.

[120] T.D. Jakes, Crushing, (FaithWords, 2019).

[121] Cindy Trimm, Hello, Tomorrow!, (Charisma House, 2018).

[122] The Erebus Story, The Loss of TE901 website, www.erebus.co.nz/.

[123] Merriam-Webster website, https://www.merriam-webster.com/dictionary/busy, https://www.merriam-webster.com/dictionary/productivity.

Chapter Thirteen: Great. Let the World See It

[124] Joel A. Barker quote from BrainyQuote website, https://www.brainyquote.com/quotes/joel_a_barker_158200.

[125] Dave Ramsey, Momentum with Sanborn, July 2012, https://open.spotify.com/episode/7b6LbRoTPnA1xSjsGUPyuC.

[126] Gary Keller with Jay Papasan, One Thing, (Bard Press, Ltd., Rellek Publishing Partners, Inc., 2012).

[127] Michael Hyatt, How to Reframe Your Fear and Let It Work for You, https://michaelhyatt.com/reframe-fear/.

[128] IDOL HISTORY IS MADE as a Contestant Walks In Off the Street to Audition - American Idol 2020, YouTube, American Idol, March 1, 2020, https://youtu.be/_c17qFtgxFw.

From My Heart to Yours

[129] How To Build Your Vision From The Ground Up | Q&A With Bishop T.D. Jakes, YouTube, Official Steven Furtick, October 26, 2017, https://youtu.be/QVGk_jwyBXI.

Overview: Grow It

[130] Zig Ziglar quote from Quotefancy website, https://quotefancy.com/quote/74320/Zig-Ziglar-Motivation-gets-you-going-and-habit-gets-you-there.

Chapter Fourteen: Iron Sharpens Iron

[131] New International Version, Bible Gateway, 1993, https://www.biblegateway.com/passage/?search=Proverbs+27%3A17&version=NIV.

[132] Napolean Hill, Think and Grow Rich, (TarcherPerigee, 2005).

Chapter Fifteen: Tools and Resources

[133] Benjamin Franklin quote from BrainyQuote website, https://www.brainyquote.com/quotes/benjamin_franklin_383997.

Afterword

[134] Alan Crozer quote from QuoteHD website, www.quotehd.com/quotes/alan-crotzer-quote-its-been-a-long-time-coming-thank-god-for-this-day.